CHRIST OUR HEALER TODAY

CONTEMPORARY THINKING on Christ's healing ministry sometimes shows a curious incongruity. The Gospel accounts of Christ's healing ministry are vigorously defended but seldom related to the present healing ministry of Christ. His healings are seen as historical, but practical only to the extent that they verify Christ's deity. The Acts and Epistles call for the continuation of healing through the church in the name of Christ.

Historically, the Alliance has been part of the nineteenth-century healing movement in America. Over 100 years, drift from healing in the Christian and Missionary Alliance is evident.

A renewal of the truth could slow drift, reverse the tide and equip our church to be a fresh voice for Christ our Healer into the twenty-first century.

CHRIST OUR HEALER TODAY

The Ministry of Healing in the Christian and Missionary Alliance

Drake W. Travis

[signature: For Drake W. Travis]

Christian Publications, Inc.
Camp Hill, Pennsylvania

Christian Publications
3825 Hartzdale Dr., Camp Hill, PA 17011
www.cpi-horizon.com

Faithful, biblical publishing since 1883

TRADE PAPER EDITION
ISBN: 0-87509-803-7
©1996 by Christian Publications, Inc.
All rights reserved
Printed in the United States of America

98 99 00 01 02   5 4 3 2 1

Graphic computerization by
Mario Liberatore and Garrett Grobler

All royalties from the sale of this book go
directly to The Great Commission Fund of
The Christian and Missionary Alliance.

To my father

URBAN VAUGHN TRAVIS
1934—

who read stories about Jesus to me
every morning for nearly 20 years

Table of Contents

Foreword

It is mysterious and lamentable that some of the simplest truths of the Christian faith have become the most complex and disunifying. For example, the "blessed hope" of Christ's return has become a divisive issue as to how Christ will come, for whom He will come, when He should come and whether the saints will experience the tribulation or be delivered from it. The details of His coming often rob us of the ineffable joy of the return itself.

Sanctification is another case in point. Are we sanctified progressively after conversion or do we become sanctified in an experience subsequent to conversion? Are we totally sanctified in an eradication of our old nature, in a life time suppression with it or in being triumphantly inhabited by the Spirit?

Divine healing, rather than a simple privilege, has also been robbed of its vitality by complex, and undoubtedly unanswerable, questions. Why do terminally ill patients linger for years and innocent children die? Why aren't all healed? Why aren't more healed? How does sovereignty intersect with prevailing prayer?

Some have answered the complex questions of healing, and nonhealing, with amazing quickness. One quick answer is that healing ended with the apostles and any attempt to project it into our time is unscriptural and ultimately cruel. Another is that God wishes to heal everyone and the only reason He usually doesn't is our failure to engage in prevailing prayer or that such prayer is emasculated by the contaminant of sin. Others just can't see that Scriptures categorically teach divine healing beyond the soul.

The result of our quest for a totally explainable divine healing is an uneasy and tentative commitment to its reality. Despite fervent prayer, too many people remain sick and too many die. In order to live with this pain and frustration, many either place healing on hold or pray lifeless, faithless prayers for people we really don't expect to get better.

Drake Travis seeks to restore our faith in divine healing. He avoids airtight solutions and treacherous extremes. Healing, he contends, is an eschatological event in which God's future victory over sickness is brought into present as an "earnest" or reminder of the total healing to come. He sees healing as a blessed gift extended by a loving God through faith and the prayers of His people. He encourages us to bring prayer out of the shadows of our faith and into practice—a joyous practice fully endorsed in God's Word.

May it be so.

David Rambo
  President, The Christian and Missionary Alliance
  President and Chairman of the Board
    National Association of Evangelicals

Acknowledgments

A project such as this requires more perseverance than one expects at the outset. It would be even more difficult were it not for the assistance of some very dear people in my life. I am grateful to:

My parents, Urb and Liz Travis, who encouraged me and gave selfless support through years of education beginning in 1966;

My wife's parents, Art and Ida Warner, who helped in finding source material and cheering me on over the long months and years;

My aunt Ruthie Travis, who encouraged me, "Drake, you must write . . .";

Jim Clements and Harry G. Tuttle of Portland, Oregon, whose graciousness helped make this endeavor possible;

Jim Maiaro and his wife, Joellen, who assisted in the research along with Karen Dashnaw, Jeff Weiss, Tom Koshy and Kevin Calvelli;

Andy Jesson, who assisted me with source material;

The kind people at Tuckahoe Alliance Church in Tuckahoe, New York, who sustained my wife and me through some very exhausting times;

All the helping hands at the Alliance Church (and the college group "Salt Co.") in Ellensburg, Washington, who helped with the surveys, tallying, word processing and editing: Mary Baxter, Stephen P. Black, Amal Daniel, Cheryl Drummond, Chad W. Duncan, Roxanne Duncan, Melissa Dyk, Sherry Dyk, Leesa L. Fookes, Sharon Graddon, Tracy Gregg, Chad Hedberg, Toni Hobbs, Bob Hoctor, Janet Isett, Nicole C. Johnson, Paul Kadlub, Serena L. Liberatore, James A. Long, Elizabeth Mirro, Joanne Mitchell, Lisa Michele Rowland, Leanne K. Ridgers, Jack Sansaver, Cindy Sholtys, Christine Simon, James Swanner, Jacqui Symonds, Heidi B. Thomas, Tammy Treit, Donna Ullman, Darryl Walsh, R.A. Young;

Garrett M. Grobler, Karen Langdon and Brian T. Wilson, the "late-night" editors;

My late cousin Ted E. Travis, (1971-1994) who helped with graphics;

Dr. Bryan Widbin, Dr. William Crockett, Dr. Leslie Andrews and Dr. Terry Wardle, who assisted in reading the drafts;

Dr. Jim Sigountos, who mentored the writing of the thesis;

Dr. Keith Bailey, who steered the transition process from thesis to book;

Mario R. Liberatore, my fellow pilgrim, who helped in countless ways—I asked him to go a mile with me . . . he went fifty;

And mostly, my dear wife Marlene, whose patience, commitment and love make the presence of God all the more real to me. Honey, I'm sorry this book took so long. How about we go back to the Bahamas for another honeymoon?

Introduction

The first grade Sunday school class at Main Street Alliance Church began its weekly warm-up activity game.

"Who makes the rain?" the teacher melodiously asked.

"Jesus!" the children chimed in unison.

"Who made the sun?"

Another gleeful "Jesus!" was heard.

"Who made the ocean?"

Once again, "Jesus!" resounded.

As the teacher posed more questions the children leaped from their seats with each "Jesus! Jesus! Jesus!" This week the teacher added a new question. "Who heals us when we are sick?"

They were silent—deathly silent.

"Who heals us when we are sick?" the teacher persisted. The children uncomfortably looked around the room wishing someone would answer. Finally little Stephanie sheepishly offered, "Medicine?"

The teacher was alarmed. I was that teacher. The incident caused me to think about the third aspect of The Christian and Missionary Alliance's fourfold gospel, "Christ our Healer." When was the last time I had heard a sermon preached on divine healing? When was the last time anyone was prayed over for divine healing? When was the last time I had seen divine healing in the Sunday school curriculum? How will these children ever know who heals us when we are sick if they are not taught?

Many feel that the third distinctive of The Christian and Missionary Alliance, "Christ Our Healer," is eroding. Leaders, parishioners, educators, members and even people outside the Alliance have made this observation. This study will examine the trend and trace of what is moving us away from healing ministry. It will also reaffirm the spiritual and biblical basis of the Alliance call to heal the sick.

Around the beginning of the 20th century, A.B. Simpson conducted a weekly healing service that was the largest midweek religious gathering in New York City. Berachah Hall, the Alliance healing home, the deeper life conferences and missionary conferences spread the message of Christ our Healer across America in the first decade of the movement. How tragic that the Alliance today does not have that same impact on the Christian community and society as a whole.

Feedback during the surveys (Appendix III) indicates that Alliance leaders see a drift from the founder's practice of healing. Of those surveyed, Alliance ministers with church and/or mission-field-based ministries, roughly 10 percent practice a healing ministry. Of the 37 biblical and theological educators surveyed from the four Alliance schools, only 10 have the definitive goal of imparting the doctrine of divine healing to their students. Twenty-two of the 37 use a curriculum void of instruction on divine healing. Nearly two-thirds of the 97 surveyed admitted that they had read very few books on divine healing.

Going with the assumption that our third distinctive is eroding, the first task is to find out why this is happening. A main reason that divine healing is neglected stems from a grave oversight in the education of our children.

Dr. Barbara Wilkerson, former professor of Christian Education at Alliance Theological Seminary, made a striking discovery while completing her doctoral studies at Rutgers University. Her dissertation was an analysis of Alliance curriculum. She found that there has been virtually no teaching of Alliance distinctives through Sunday school material since the 1940's. In the 1940's The Christian and Missionary Alliance stopped writing its own Sunday school curriculum and began to purchase it from an evangelical publisher. There has not been systematic and compelling instruction about Christ as our Healer since. This would do anything but keep the Alliance distinctives fresh in people's minds. There are now second generation adults in The Christian and Missionary Alliance leaders who have not been regularly taught that Christ is our Savior, Sanctifier, Healer and Coming King. As illustrated in the opening story, the third generation is following close behind.

In a personal interview conducted at headquarters in April 1989, Christian and Missionary Alliance journalist Bob Niklaus shared the reasons he thinks healing is not widely practiced in Alliance churches as it once was.[1]

Niklaus said one reason healing has not retained its significance is that Simpson's perspective of divine healing ran much deeper than most people's. Simpson saw "Christ Our Healer" as a consequence of abiding in Christ. His view was like that of Paul who says in Romans 8:11, "[H]e who raised Christ from the dead will also give life to your mortal bodies through his Spirit, who lives in you." This, in turn, pushes out the old life of self. And as salvation was a truth for one's entire being, so were sanctification and healing. Niklaus stated that this view became difficult to maintain after Simpson had passed on.

The second reason is that most people have a "body parts" idea about healing. They want God to fix their arm, their wrist, their ear or lymph glands. Simpson wanted people wholly sanctified. And that was a much more involving issue than the mere physical healing that most wanted. Simpson's view of healing requires a piercing vision of godliness.

The third reason, according to Niklaus, for the decline in Alliance healing ministry is the fear created by charismatic exploitation.

The attitude of some Christians toward the reality of spiritual warfare tends to erode their interest in healing. Deliverance from demonic influence is related to the practice of divine healing. That does not mean all illness has its origin in the demonic; it simply means deliverance from demonization in its various forms is an aspect of healing. Some people fear this encounter with the powers of darkness and therefore neglect healing.

Many dismiss the matter of healing because of an unhappy experience with the practice of this teaching. Some have attempted to believe for healing and they perceived that effort to be a failure. Perhaps they prayed for a loved one who did not recover. The error in this response is the disregard of the Scriptures. Promises and instruction for the ministry of healing are undeniably a part of the Word of God.

Contemporary thinking on Christ's healing ministry sometimes shows a curious incongruity. The gospel accounts of Christ's healing ministry are vigorously defended but never related to the present healing ministry of Christ. His healings are seen as historical, but practical only to the extent that they verify Christ's deity. The Acts and Epistles call for the continuation of healing through the Church in the name of Christ.

Historically, the Alliance has been part of the 19th century healing movement in America. Over 100 years, drift from healing in The Christian and Missionary Alliance is evident. A renewal of the truth could slow the drift, reverse the tide and equip our church to be a fresh voice for Christ our Healer into the 21st century.

The re-examination of the biblical evidence for divine healing would be a good beginning. Along with biblical study, a serious look at the literature of The Christian and Missionary Alliance on this doctrine and the literature of many other evangelical church bodies would help us to regain an understanding of this biblical doctrine. This study has as its objective a call to renewal of the ministry of divine healing in our day on a comprehensive and international level.

Endnotes

1. Robert L. Niklaus, interviewed by author, Nyack, New York, 18 April 1989.

Chapter 1

Healing in the Old Testament

The truth of physical healing as an act of God in response to faith and prayer is found throughout the Scripture. The theology and the principle of divine healing are first set forth in the Old Testament.

The Old Testament Concept of Man

The Old Testament concept of man came from God by revelation. To the Hebrew, man was a whole harmonious unit. This perception contrasts with Greek thought on the nature of man. The Greeks saw man comprised of many parts frequently at war with each other, the body being one of them. In Greek thinking, man's body was perceived as evil. To the Hebrew, the body was not evil.

The Hebrew was constantly conscious of the One True God and the Law He had given them. God's Law dealt with every aspect of life. This consciousness of the Law carried into every activity, occupation, business deal, relationship, meal, health condition, thought, act of worship and emotion. Under God, life was interrelated like a networked computer system is today. Such a relationship called for total dedication to God in obedience and worship.

The Old Testament/Hebrew concept of wholeness was God-centered. It guarded the Hebrew against the spiritual, physical and emotional imbalances that plague people in the modern day world. The Word of God provided a complete program of guidance in the best interest of the whole man.

The Hebrew Idea of Health

The biblical concept of "wholeness" included health. The Hebrew cherished health as a blessing from God. Good health was equated with having one's entire life in order. When one's heart, soul, mind and body were functioning well that person was considered to be blessed by God.

Conversely, in the Old Testament era, sickness was not seen as a great perplexity, but as part of God's intervention in life. There was no question as to whether one should call on God in time of illness. Sickness was a call to prayer and spiritual renewal. In fact, it was sin to not call on God in times of physical need. In Second Kings 1, Ahaziah died because he did not call on God when he was injured, but called on the god of Ekron.

"Wholeness" was the root idea of holiness according to the book of Leviticus. Gordon Wenham, in his commentary *The Book of Leviticus*, explains the Hebrew concept of "wholeness."[1] He draws from the studies of Mary Douglas, a social anthropologist, who offers a sound interpretation of the *kosher* system and how it contributed to wholeness. The *kosher* system was in compliance with the laws of separation found in Leviticus.

It gave comprehensive instruction for diet, relationships, health care and many other guidelines for everyday living. The *kosher* system applied not only to wholeness, which indicates completeness, but also to holiness, which refers to purity. Separation unto God was basic to a life of completeness, balance and worship. Therefore, anything presented in the Temple had to be without flaw, perfect and whole. Anyone approaching the Temple to make an offering had to be clean and free of any bodily discharges (either from a membrane or an open sore).

The *kosher* theme of separation affected every area of life. To combine certain things was perversion. Mixing symbolized confusion. There was to be no mixing of the holy and the unholy. In terms of religion, they had one God and no other. In marriage, adultery was forbidden; it was mixing. In agriculture only one type of grain was to be planted in a field. Relationships were to be forthright and honest whether they were social or business. God's Word condemned deceptive dealing in one's public or private life. The Hebrews were to separate themselves from anything that hinted of duplicity.

Leviticus also lays out the dietary plan for wholeness. Meat from land, air or sea creatures could be eaten. The regulations were as follows: A land animal must chew the cud and have a split hoof to be *kosher*. Only flying creatures that had two wings and two feet were *kosher*. And only creatures of the sea that had fins and scales were *kosher*. Any creature with mixed characteristics was not to be eaten. For example, pigs, camels, most insects, eels (the list is extensive) were unclean. Pigs have split hooves but do not chew cud. Camels chew cud but do not have split hooves. Most insects have multiple legs, and eels have a fin but no scales. According to Douglas, these were forbidden because they symbolize mixing and not wholeness. Carnivorous scavengers and things that flew in swarms versus patterns were creatures of confusion and madness, therefore unclean.

The food laws had a greater purpose than intestinal hygiene. Through this law the Israelites were ever distinguishing clean from unclean. It kept the subject of holiness and integrity foremost in their hearts.

The main lesson from Leviticus was that wholeness was an important aspect of true holiness. The Hebrews were to experience this *shalom* wholeness in their faith, their homes, their bodies, their relationships and society. They were to avoid anything contrary to wholeness. The wholeness presented in Leviticus included God's gift of health. To enjoy this health, Israel must remain true to God in covenant with Him.

Healing as Part of the Covenant

One of the benefits to those following the stipulations of the covenant was health and strength. The Lord promised this to the Israelites. All they had to do was carefully obey the Law as given through Moses. Health would then result, just as surely as pain and suffering would result from disobedience. These were their two options.

1. Obedience vs. Disobedience

Shortly after Israel crossed the Red Sea, the Lord gave the promise of healing to His people (Exodus 15:26-27). God said that if they obeyed His commandments they would be exempt from the diseases that plagued the Egyptians. "From this point on, Israel was to understand that their physical well being was dependent upon abiding in the redemptive covenant."[2] God alone was their healer. This was "a matter not of feeling or religious inclination, but a fact."[3] The contract for the future was very clear. The blessing of healing was associated with obedience to God's Word.

Moses, in Deuteronomy 28, explained the conditions of covenant blessing to Israel. On the one hand, God assured consummate blessing for obedience. Their status, children, livestock, food, travels, weather and even political situations would be established in blessing. On the other hand, disobedience would bring on a nightmare of disaster. (Sickness is one of the curses sent upon the disobedient.) Diseases, fever, inflammation, blight, boils, tumors, festering sores, madness, blindness and insanity would plague them. These "plagues" were a judgment of God according to the prophets. Prophets writing during the years of national rebellion, refer to the threat of "plague" 36 times. In short, the LORD required obedience as the avenue to health and wholeness.

> The whole future of Israel depended on faithful obedience to the law of God. Thus the long and solemn sermon on the curses of God provides a final incentive for whole-hearted commitment in renewing the covenant.[4]

The ways of the LORD stood ominously before them: Obey God or wither and die.

Neither at the beginning nor at any point in their journey were the Israelites perfect in obedience. God sometimes used sickness as a corrective measure with them. "The purpose of inflicting the sickness was to get at the underlying spiritual condition."[5]

One instance where sickness is seen (from a human standpoint) as God's judgment is in First Kings 17:7ff. Elijah visits the widow at Zarephath. After several incidents take place her son dies. She interprets the death as punishment for her sin. Elijah arrives, and she says, "What do you have against me, man of God? Did you come to remind me of my sin and kill my son?" (17:18).

Many years later this covenant was reaffirmed by Solomon in his prayer of dedication for the Temple (2 Chronicles 6:14-42). He petitioned God to hear the prayer of those afflicted by diseases and to heal them. "The sufferer could only look to God, the Physician of his people, for healing and recovery."[6]

2. Healing as Part of Redemption

The Old Testament treats physical healing as an integral part of God's redemption. "Since God was the physician of his people, it followed that healing constituted a manifest token of his forgiveness."[7]

One might note that when healing was a manifestation of forgiveness, some ritual was required in order for the supplicant to experience healing. One example is in Numbers 21:4-9. The Israelites had received deadly snakebites because of their complaining. To be forgiven of their complaining they were required to look at a bronze snake that Moses was instructed to put on a pole. Healing was simultaneous.

Similar situations are recorded in Numbers 16:47 and Second Kings 20:7. In the former, Aaron offers incense, and a plague is halted immediately. In the latter, figs are applied to Hezekiah's boil and he recovers. This is how God involved people in the process of forgiveness and healing with looking.

Healing provided a powerful reason to rejoice and praise God. It also renewed a person's commitment to the covenant. There were times when even those who were not Hebrew, part of the covenant, would praise God in the highest for divine healing. One impressive example is Nebuchadnezzar of Babylon. He is struck with insanity because of his pride. At the moment of his healing, he replies:

> Then I praised the Most High; I honored and glorified him who lives forever.
> His dominion is an eternal dominion; his kingdom endures from generation to generation. All the peoples of the earth are regarded as nothing. He does as he pleases with the powers of heaven and the peoples of the earth. No one can hold back his hand or say to him: "What have you done?" . . . Now I, Nebuchadnezzar, praise and exalt and glorify the King of heaven, because everything he does is right and all his ways are just. And those who walk in pride he is able to humble. (Daniel 4:34b-35, 37)

It was the common assumption that forgiveness and healing went together. Just as forgiveness caused a renewal of relationship with God, so did its tangent reality, the healing of the physical body. R.K. Harrison has stated that "because sickness was a spiritual matter, in the last analysis, healing could only properly be expected to follow a revival or revitalizing of the relationship between the individual and God."[8] As surely as God used sickness to bring attention to sin, He used healing to restore joy.

God the Unchanging Healer

The biblical fact of God's immutability also covers the biblical fact that God heals His people. God states that He is the Healer of His people in Exodus 15. He does not withdraw this statement. Therefore "God as Healer" must be perceived as an established institution that He keeps, not a theological phase that He passes through. The Old Testament describes God as Healer, and as such, He is immutable as He is in all of His offices.

1. Yahweh-Rapha (Exodus 15:26)

When God gave His word to the Israelites after crossing the Red Sea He told them not to fear disease, but keep the covenant because "I am your healer [(your) *rapha*]." In other words, God was telling them that He could and would fix any problem they had, so they must remain in relationship with Him. He was their completely capable Great Physician. This declaration testified to a definite office He held and a power that He dispatched.

This is significant because it is not an action that God is doing for merely a season. The statement, "I am the LORD, who heals you . . ." is not a temporary blessing but a proclamation of lasting theological import. God is eternal.

2. God's Immutability

Malachi 3:6 says, "I the LORD do not change." God is perfect; He does not need to change, learn or grow. His power does not decline nor does He lose His attributes. He is an unchanging God. This goes for healing. Yet "it is strange how many

15

people think of God as the 'I was' "[9] It was not so in the days of the Old Testament. They took God at His word to be their Healer. They were taught this from their distinctive beginning through the time of Malachi and into the intertestamental period.

To their knowledge it was God's plan to heal them. Psalm 33:11 says, "[T]he plans of the LORD stand firm forever." The psalmist, no doubt, knew God as the Healer. Psalm 102:27 reads, "But you remain the same, and your years will never end." Malachi, whose work closes out the Old Testament, gave the final promises for better days: "But for you who revere my name, the sun of righteousness will rise with healing in its wings. And you will go out and leap like calves released from the stall" (Malachi 4:2).

Despite the fact that the Old Testament reiterates that God is a healing God, there are present-day theologies that void out God as the Healer (*Yahweh-Rapha*). Modern existentialism, for one, eradicates this promise that God Himself made over 3,000 years ago. Oswald J. Smith asks, "If He is not *Jehovah-rapha*, then how can I be sure that He is still *Jehovah-tsidkenu* [the Lord our Righteousness] or *Jehovah-jireh* [the Lord who sees]? When did He change?"[10] The absurdity of the question insists that He never did and never will change.

Biblical Healing in the Old Testament Era

There are many references to and incidents of

divine healing in the Old Testament text. Healing is seen in propositional statements and promises. The historical Word gives incidents of healing. From the Pentateuch to the prophets, the Bible gives the record of God healing His people. This usually accompanied spiritual healing as well. Keith Bailey asserts that "the truth of divine healing is a part of the theology of the Old Testament. The historical, the poetical, and the prophetic books—all teach healing for the saints."[11]

The Main References about Healing

Sometimes Christians think healing began with the earthly ministry of Christ. But a study of the Old Testament shows that the experience of divine healing among God's people began in Old Testament times.

1. God Himself as Healer

The initial reference to God Himself as a Healer is found in Exodus 15:26. It reads, "I am the LORD, who heals you." The Israelites had witnessed the entire nation of Egypt inflicted with calamity and diseases prior to leaving. Now on the opposite side of the Red Sea, the dramatic escape was accomplished; Egypt's army had drowned right behind them and though they were awestruck and overjoyed, they stood in need of comfort and assurance. Within three days of the Exodus, God promised them that the horrible diseases they had seen in Egypt would not come upon them. God Himself was their Healer and

17

they could rely on Him. This was not only an action He would perform but an office He upheld. In other words, He and no one else was their Physician. "Being [Yahweh], or their reconciled God, He, of necessity, is also their Healer."[12] It was the first of a long series of lessons.

The instruction was that His people were to come to Him for everything, to view all of life in reference to Him. Exodus 23:25-26 reads:

> Worship the LORD your God, and his blessing will be on your food and water. I will take away sickness from among you, and none will miscarry or be barren in your land. I will give you a full life span.

In following God there was provision, health, security for the young, old and unborn: basic womb-to-tomb protection.

In Deuteronomy 32:39 Moses is preaching to all Israel, preparing them to enter the land of promise. On behalf of God he says, "I put to death and I bring to life, I have wounded and I will heal." This is within his final reminder before he views the land, blesses the tribes and dies. They must never forget that God does and will heal.

In Isaiah 42 God speaks through His servant whom He upholds, has chosen, delights in, will put His Spirit on and who will bring justice to the nations (42:1). This same servant opens the eyes of the blind (42:7). In Isaiah 57:18-19 God makes a promise to the contrite in heart:

"I have seen his ways, but I will heal him; I will guide him and restore comfort to him, creating praise on the lips of the mourners in Israel. Peace, peace, to those far and near," says the LORD. "And I will heal them."

Jeremiah, in 30:16ff., is speaking to a broken nation when God tells His people that the captivity, oppression and pain will end. He assures, "I will restore you to health and heal your wounds," (30:17). In Jeremiah 33 the Lord speaks about Judah and Israel being restored. In 33:6 He says, "Nevertheless, I will bring health and healing to it; I will heal my people and will let them enjoy abundant peace and security."

Lastly, Hosea 11:3 reads, "It was I who taught Ephraim to walk, taking them by the arms; but they did not realize it was I who healed them."

In each of the above passages, except Exodus 23, the Hebrew word *rapha* or its root is used. *Rapha* basically means to sew together what has been torn apart. God is the self-proclaimed Healer who puts back together what has been torn.

2. The Classic Passages of Psalm 103 and Isaiah 53

Psalm 103 shines as a psalm that testifies to God's all-encompassing care and goodness. It is the first of a group of five praise psalms that were used in worship services of thanksgiving. The setting is that a singer would voice the sentiments of an entire congregation.

For some, the crippling handicap of sin had earlier manifested itself in illness. Now, thank God, it had been removed by healing, which was the outward sign of his [God's] gracious forgiveness. He had proved their champion, rescuing them from Sheol's premature clutches.[13]

In verse 2 of Psalm 103 is the reminder not to forget the benefits of the Lord. These benefits are spelled out in vv. 3-6. He forgives all sins, heals all diseases, redeems life from the pit, crowns His own with love and compassion, satisfies desires with good things, renews youth like the eagle's and works righteousness and justice for all the oppressed. The seven verbs listed above are ample reason to praise the Lord. According to Psalm 103, "The blessing of healing includes recovery from disease, deliverance from the grave, and renewal of physical vigor."[14] Nothing else was needed to enjoy an abundant life in God.

Verse 3 upholds the Old Testament belief that forgiveness of sin and healing of disease are wedded blessings. These two blessings are grammatically paralleled in the Hebrew text. In this passage it does not say that He heals certain diseases, or diseases up to a point, but that He heals "all your diseases" (103:3). Any healing that took place anywhere, from the time of Adam to the time of Malachi, was the work of the Lord.

Isaiah 53 is one of the most powerful healing passages in the Old Testament. It speaks of the es-

sence of One who is to be a Savior: His work, His
suffering and the meaning of it all.

> Surely he took up our infirmities
>   and carried our sorrows,
> yet we considered him stricken by God,
>   smitten by him, and afflicted.
> But he was pierced for our
>   transgressions,
>   he was crushed for our iniquities;
> the punishment that brought us peace was
>   upon him,
>   and by his wounds we are healed.
>   (53:4-5)

"Our infirmities" refers to being frail physically; "our sorrows" refers to being frail emotion-
ally. A.B. Simpson comments that the same
Hebrew word used here for infirmities is translated "sickness" roughly 100 other times in the
Old Testament (the King James Version). "Infirmities" also refers to disease. Any worthy transla-
tion of this first phrase in verse 4 denotes it as any
sort of ailment. "Although the figure of sicknesses
here used refers to sin itself, the verse also includes the thought of the removal of the consequences of sin. Disease is the inseparable
companion of sin."[15] These ailments "he takes
up." The "sorrows" that He carries are what are
precipitated by the ailments: results of the infirmities. One catches the implication that Isaiah is setting forth. Pain is not only suffering, but the fact

that disease often lingers to bring on an anguish and sorrow all its own, resulting in heartbreak and the eventual crushing of the person's spirit. One example is a 20th century polio victim who has said that the worst part about having to live with braces and crutches is the depression.

The suffering servant lifts all this. "It should be noted that the consequences of sin and not sin itself are mentioned. Nevertheless, when it is said that He bore our sicknesses, what is meant is . . . that He bore the sin that is the cause of the evil consequences."[16] Informal English uses phrases such as "down with the flu" or "under the weather" to mean one is being held down by sickness. Isaiah employs the same word usage in saying that this is lifted away. The two verbs for "taking up" and "carrying" in Hebrew are *nasa* and *sabal*. "The former implies not only the taking of it, but bearing of it away; and the latter emphasizes the weight of the load."[17] Isaiah speaks of the perfect, the necessary and the comprehensive remedy. By this remedy the illness is removed, and the spirit that was withered away because of illness is completely restored.

Nasa and *sabal* are not only words of healing and restoration, they are sacrificial terms. They speak of one being used to carry something for another. Note the motif of the elevation process. For example, Othniel in Judges 3:7-11 is a deliverer who is "raised up for them" (3:9). He returned the nation to a state of peace. Moses ministered healing when he made a bronze snake and "put it up on a pole"

(Numbers 21:8-9). Jesus alluded to this lifting process in John 3:14. The lifting of Himself would be similar to the lifting of the serpent. Note that in a sacrifice the smoke rises up to the Lord and is pleasing to Him. And it is the result of lifting up Jesus as a sacrifice that would be the ultimate and final healing unto eternal life for all who believe.

The lifting and carrying away of our sickness and sorrow is not some vague hope. Isaiah 53:4 begins, "Surely he took up. . . ." The Hebrew word for "surely" is *akhen*. The *Brown-Driver-Briggs Hebrew-English Lexicon* defines *akhen* as "surely, truly; an adverb with strong assertive force" (p. 38). They continue, ". . . expressing the reality, in opposition to what had been wrongly imagined." A.B. Simpson asserts, "The only 'surely' in the chapter is the promise of healing, the very strongest possible statement of complete redemption from pain and sickness by His life and death."[18]

Simpson also says in *The Lord for the Body*, "[I]t is an underlining of the passage intended to mark it as very important . . . not only important but absolutely true."[19] What is stressed is the certainty of substitution. One is suffering so others do not have to.

From the grammar it is impossible to conclude that this substitutionary sacrifice applies only to sin and not to sickness. All agree that God forgives and removes sin. But some think that this Scriptural reference to alleviating human pain is to be spiritualized. However, a careful look at the passage shows that to spiritualize healing does not agree with Old Testament theology. Isaiah describes the full benefits of the suffering servant's death. As mentioned above, all agree that substitution for sin has been made. Isaiah 53:12c reads, "For he bore the sin of many." This is clear theologically. Isaiah employs the same word used for the sacrifice for sin to describe what was done to infirmities, sicknesses and diseases. One must conclude, then, that He lifted away both sin and sicknesses. To say "By his stripes we are healed" just means spiritual healing is tautology [senseless repetition].[20] Along with the spiritual healing of Isaiah 53, physical healing is clearly offered in verses 4 and 5. Dare we take God's gracious gifts to us and dismiss them through spiritualizing oblivion?

The Old Testament Concept of Health (A Lexical Survey)

To "see it like a Hebrew" one must look more closely at the Hebrew words for such related terms as healing and health—how and where they are used as God originally defined it for the Israelites.

1. The Hebrew Definitions of Healing

In the Hebrew text of the Old Testament, *rapha* is the word most commonly used to denote healing. *Rapha* is defined in *The New Brown-Driver-Briggs Hebrew and English Lexicon* (1979) as "heal," "mend," "repair," "pacify," "stitch together." Several different forms and stems of *rapha* are employed.

24

The verb *rapha* initially refers to the healing or general correction of a physical situation. It means to restore something that is in a state of disrepair. This always refers to something tangible, even though it may have direct spiritual or emotional ramifications. *Rapha* means to restore something to its original state. But *Brown-Driver-Briggs* includes "pacify" within its definition. Most humans understand the pacifying effect of having a situation returned to normalcy. Anxiety then dissipates and peace returns. There are many settings in the Old Testament where *rapha* refers to the repair of bodily ailments. One is found in Numbers 12:13. Here Moses cries out to God on behalf of Miriam who had become white with leprosy; "God please heal her!" He wanted her to be as she had been before. In Second Kings 20, Hezekiah is at the point of death when God promises that He will heal him (20:5). And Naaman is restored from leprosy in Second Kings 5.

The Old Testament teaches that God works *rapha* on the national level as well. God performs *rapha* in three intersecting ways: first, by forgiving sin and reversing its effects; second, by curing disease as just discussed; and third, by restoring the nation in demise.

There are at least six key verses that refer to the healing *(rapha)* of sin on the national level. Second Chronicles 7:14 states that if they will turn from their wicked ways, God will heal their land. According to Second Chronicles 30:20, Hezekiah prayed and the people were healed (made ceremonially clean) for the Passover. Isaiah 57:17-19 promises healing of sinful greed and the punishment it brings. Jeremiah speaks of Israel cured (*rapha*) of backsliding (Jeremiah 3:22). He also predicted that God would heal wicked Judah (Jeremiah 36:6ff). God will heal Israel's waywardness according to Hosea 14:4.

Rapha is needed to restore the nation of Israel after terror, crushing and horror in Jerusalem (Jeremiah 8:15ff). The people are longing for peace and a time of healing—"healing for the wound of my people" (Jeremiah 8:22). Jeremiah 30:16-17 refers to plundering enemies coming to loot and destroy. " '*But* (italics mine) I will restore . . . and heal your wounds,' declares the LORD."

Rapha is also used to fix anything in a condition of disrepair. In First Kings 18:30 Elijah repairs (*rapha*) the altar of the Lord, "which was in ruins." The New International Version of the Bible translates the verb here "he repaired. . . ." The altar in ruins testified to Israel's state of spiritual decline. So *rapha* means to put back together that which has fallen apart or disintegrated. For it is God's nature to work *rapha* in people's bodies as well as for the nations, healing sin, disease and ruin.

The Hebrew word *rapha* also applies to the distresser of the individual. For instance, Jeremiah was oppressed, scorned and rejected by his contemporaries. Crushed in spirit and in despair he says to God, "Heal me, O LORD, and I will be healed" (Jeremiah 17:14). The psalmist, in 41:4, weighed down with sin and being slandered by his enemies, says, "O Lord, have mercy on me; heal me." Psalm 147:3 also helps us understand this definition of *rapha*. It reads, "He heals the brokenhearted and binds up their wounds." God takes people with all their emotional and psychological distresses and puts them back together again.

There is a series of derivations from *rapha* that have the connotation of nursing back to health. In this case *rapha* applies to man's participation in the healing process. In Hebrew grammar this is the reflexive stem.

In Second Kings 8:29 (and Second Chronicles 22:6) "King Joram returned to Jezreel to *recover* from the wounds" In this passage *rapha* means "convalescence." *Rapha* in the Hithpael (H-stem) carries the meaning of a "remedy." This is found in Ezekiel 30:21 where a broken arm did not heal because it was not bound or put in a splint. The New International Version actually translates *rapha* as "remedy" in Jeremiah 30:13 and 46:11. It signifies a healing medicine of some sort.

The purpose of healing (*rapha*) is so that life may continue. When *rapha* occurs the ensuing power of death itself is halted. This is seen in Second Kings 2:21-22 where water from a well is making the land unproductive and causing death. Elijah puts salt in the well and the well is "healed," no longer causing death to plants and people. Again in Ezekiel 47:9 water is healed so that fish can live. "This water flows there makes the salt water fresh."

Finally, there is the word *raphoat* which is related to *rapha*. Meaning "health" in the general sense of that term, it is similar to English where "th" is added to turn the verb "heal" into the noun "health."

Another interesting Hebrew word is *marpe*. *Brown-Driver-Briggs* defines it as "healing," "cure" and "health." It is distinctive in that it deals more with the state of healing than with the process. Brown, Driver and Briggs listed three areas of healing covered by *marpe*. (These are similar to *rapha*.) *Marpe* is used for the healing of national woes. It can indicate health and profit for a person and for the healing of disease in one's physical frame.

Jeremiah used this word in 14:19 in relationship to Israel's problems. It reads, "We hoped for peace but no good has come, for a time of healing but there is only terror." Here *marpe* refers to a curative for catastrophic situations. In Jeremiah 14:19, with Judah predicted to fall victim to both sword and famine, Jeremiah asks God, "Why have you afflicted us so that we cannot be healed?"

In Proverbs the writer uses *marpe* to express health and prosperity (Proverbs 4:22; 12:18; 13:17 and 16:24). These passages are about wholeness. They say, "[Listening to wisdom is] health to a man's whole body." "The tongue of the wise brings healing." "A trustworthy envoy brings healing." And "pleasant words are . . . healing to the bones."

Marpe also speaks to the state of those who seek healing. It is found in Malachi 4:2 wherein healing is promised to those who fear the name of the LORD Almighty. In Proverbs 14:30 *laiv marpe* is translated, "a heart at peace." Peace of heart is conducive to good health. In Ecclesiastes 10:4 *marpe* is translated "calmness" and, like peace, it aids healing.

Another word for "healing" in the Old Testament is *te-alah*, which has the general meaning of new flesh over a wound. It is used exclusively for healing. In the context of Jeremiah 30:13 there is much talk about wounds, injuries and pain. The Lord says, "There is . . . no healing for you." In both references they are simply left to bleed. That is, wounds will remain open wounds.

Te-alah is also the word for "conduit" or "watercourse." This is a graphic metaphor of a trench of some sort. And with this same term meaning "healing," it is then considered to express healing for a trench-like incision in the flesh. *Te-alah* is actually to dress a wound, and by doing so stop the flow of blood.

The word *arukhah* (accent on third syllable) refers to the healing of a wound, the new flesh that grows at the wounded spot. As for health, it carries the sense of healing as a restoration.

Isaiah 58:8 promises, "your healing will quickly appear (*arukhah*)." God laid down conditions for receiving the promise of healing. They were to act in justice, clothe the naked and cease from turning away their own flesh and blood. In Second Chronicles 24:13 *arukhah* is translated "repairs." The Temple, in need of reinforcement and restoration, is being repaired. *Arukhah* is translated "restore" in Jeremiah 30:17. The Lord will "restore" them to health. Jeremiah 33:6 uses *arukhah* along with *marpe* and *rapha* in this verse about healing. It reads "I will bring health (*arukhah*) and healing (*marpe*) to it; I will heal (*rapha*) my people and will let them enjoy abundant peace and security." The context shows the wound, too, is sin and it must be remedied before people can return to God and enjoy His peace. Jeremiah brings both spiritual and physical healing together in this verse.

The word *subh* (pronounced "shoove," rhymes with "groove") is a Hebrew word for healing that means "restore." *Subh* refers specifically to the process of bringing back. *Brown-Driver-Briggs* defines *subh* "to return." In the area of health it means a returning from bad to good health. For example, Job 33:25 discusses one's flesh being restored as in the days of youth.

Often translated "return," it expresses healing in spiritual relationships. Hosea 6:1 says, "Come, let us return to the LORD." Returning is part of the healing process. Hosea 14:2 urges Israel to return to the LORD for forgiveness and healing. In First Kings 8, Solomon is praying for the people, that Israel might return to the LORD for healing and restoration (see 8:33ff). Returning is a paramount factor in the theology of healing. In the quest for healing, repentance was required. Isaiah speaks of the reconciliation and healing that results from returning to God.

Restoration leads to refreshment. It is in this sense that Psalm 23:3 uses *subh*. David says, "[H]e restores my soul." (He returns David's soul to where it should be.) Proverbs 25:13c says, "He refreshes the spirit. . . ." We can see how God returns (*subh*) people to spiritual health. In Isaiah 58:12c those who are rebuilding the walls are called "Restorer [*subh* is a participial noun] of Streets with Dwellings." Daniel prophesied to restore (*subh*) Jerusalem (Daniel 9:25).

Alah, which literally means "to bring up" in terms of new flesh, is ordinarily a sacrificial form, but it also applied to physical healing.

The psalmist has seen many troubles but displays his confidence in 71:20: "[F]rom the depths of the earth you will again bring me up." Jeremiah 30:17 assured, "I will restore you to health." God lifted Israel back up to where He wished they would stay. And again, in the "healing-laden" verse, Jeremiah 33:6, Jeremiah writes, "I will bring health (*alah*) and healing" (*Alah* is a participle in this verse.) Lamentations 5:21b reads, "[R]enew our days as of old." "Renew" is a stem of *alah*. It is a prayer that the nation be brought up again to where it once was.

The word *qum* means "to arise" or "stand." It refers to rising from the dead. An example is found in Second Kings 13:21, where the dead man is thrown into Elisha's tomb. "When the body touched Elisha's bones, the man came to life and stood up (*qum*) on his feet." Isaiah 26:19 promises, "But your dead will live; their bodies will rise (*qum*)."

Old Testament healing includes ideas like "restore to life," "revive," "quicken," "refresh" and "preserve." The corresponding word in Hebrew is *hayah*. An example of *hayah* is found in First Samuel 2:6: "The Lord brings death and makes alive." The same thought is found in Deuteronomy 32:39, "I put to death and I bring to life." King Hezekiah thanked God when his life was spared. He rejoices before God in Isaiah 38:16 and prays, "You restored me to health and let me live." *Hayah* is used in the incident where Elisha revived the young boy to life again.

Isaiah 57:15 testifies to God's power to revive (*hayah*): "I live . . . with him who is contrite and lowly in spirit, to revive the spirit of the lowly and to revive the heart of the contrite." And Psalm 119 speaks repeatedly of how God's Word revives. In this chapter the Word of God has the power of *hayah*, translated to mean "the preservation of life" (see 51:25, 37, 40, 50, 88, 93, 107, 149, 154, 156, 159). *Brown-Driver-Briggs* also gives *hayah* the meaning "to be quickened," meaning revived from sickness, discouragement, faintness or death (p. 310a).

The words *hadash* and *halaph* are translated "heal" in the New International Version. Both words literally mean "to renew." First, for *hadash*, it is used in Second Chronicles 15:8 when Asa repaired (*hadash*) the altar of the LORD. Nine chapters later in 24:4 Joash is gathering money to repair (*hadash*) the Temple. This same concept is in Isaiah 61:4b: "[T]hey will renew the ruined cities." In Psalm 51:12 (51:10 in the New International Version) David prays that God would renew a steadfast spirit within him.

Later in Psalm 103:5 the benefits of the Lord are summarized with the renewing of youth like the eagle's. Psalm 104:30 praises God's Spirit who makes all creation and renews (*hadash*) the face of the earth. This *hadash* is an all-encompassing work, making new temples, altars, cities, man's spirit, man's youth and vitality and ultimately the face of the whole earth.

Halaph is used in Isaiah 40:31 which reads, "[T]hose who hope in the LORD will renew (*halaph*) their strength." The King James Version, from which the popular song is written, reads, "[T]hey that wait upon the LORD shall renew their strength." The body is strengthened when they seek the Lord. Isaiah 41:1 commands, "Let the nations renew their strength!" Renewal comes with placing one's hope in the Lord. God has displayed His omnipotent power to heal the sick in the Old Testament. The near-dozen Hebrew words paint the portrait of God our Healer.

2. Shalom: The Hebrew Concept of Health

When God makes sick people well He also gives them rest. In some instances, God disrupted people's lives to put them at peace again. *Shalom* has been described as "a state of well-being in which nothing essential is lacking."[21] This *shalom* means one has ample resources and the heart/soul/mind/body are in harmony. Surely God is present in that situation.

Shalom is an abstract noun. Its general definition, according to *Brown-Driver-Briggs*, is "completeness," "soundness," "welfare" and "peace." *Brown-Driver-Briggs* goes on to define the word with six subdivisions to more fully explain its meaning.

First, *shalom* means "completeness" as in the peace and rest we experience when a task has just been completed. Second, *shalom* means "safety" and "soundness." David laments in Psalm 38:3, "[M]y bones have no soundness because of my sin." His body, because of his spirit, was apparently becoming scarecrow-like. Job 5:24 translates *shalom* "secure" when Eliphaz replies, "You will know that your tent is secure." One can see the illustration given: Ropes are taut, stakes are driven deep, poles high and in place. Scripturally speaking, man lives in *shalom*, "secure" when he is safe and sound, when everything is in place.

Third, *shalom* means "welfare," "health," " prosperity." This third aspect is twofold. First, it is a statement regarding general welfare. It signifies whether one is "OK" or not. *Shalom* is found twice in Genesis 43:27. The New International Version reads: "He asked them how they were, and then he said, 'How is your aged father you told me about?' " In Jeremiah 38:4 "the good of these people" is their *shalom*. In this definition, *shalom* is equivalent to the American English greeting, "How are you doing?"

This aspect also hints more directly of physical health and wellness. For example, in Genesis 29:6 Jacob asks of Laban, "Is he well?" i.e., is he "in *shalom*"? In Second Samuel 18:28 is the greeting, "All is well!" The context of Second Kings 4:26 is the

Shunnamite's son being restored to life. Gehazi used *shalom* four times as he inquired about the whole family.

Fourth, *shalom* means "peace," "quiet," "tranquility," "contentment." This is a peace that is both national and personal. Isaiah 32:17 says, "The fruit of righteousness will be peace." What follows is quietness and confidence. Psalm 4:8 says "I will lie down and sleep in peace." It is a peace that allows one to depart from this life in tranquility. God assures Abram in Genesis 15:15, "You, however, will go to your fathers in peace and be buried at a good old age." In First Kings 2:6 the wicked are seen without peace at death. Isaiah 32:18 prophesies, "My people will live in peaceful dwelling places, in secure homes, in undisturbed places of rest." Peace, security, quiet contentment—it is all *shalom*.

Fifth, *shalom* is peace in terms of friendship. It is peace with other humans. Genesis 26:29, 31 tells of the peace established between Isaac and Abimelech. Psalm 35:20 talks about those who live quietly in the land. There is harmony with the neighbors. Those who promote peace have joy according to Proverbs 12:20. *Shalom* in terms of man-to-man relationships is the harmony necessary in human society.

This definition of *shalom* also describes peace with both God and man. In Numbers 25:12 the Lord is making a covenant of peace with the Israelites. Isaiah 53:5b, says "[T]he punishment that brought us peace was upon him, and by his wounds we are healed." The penalty of sin having been paid by the suffering servant, man's relationship with God is restored and man is offered peace and healing. In Isaiah 54:10 the Lord assures of His love and covenant of peace: *shalom*. This *shalom* is referred to again in Malachi 2:5-6.

Finally, *shalom* is peace from war. Leviticus 25:6 promises that there will be peace in the land if they are obedient. The Old Testament discusses of a time when peace will be ultimate. Isaiah 9:6 says that the child born is the Prince of Peace. As He comes to rule His ever-increasing government, peace will be universal. This will be *shalom* without end or borders. Micah 5:4, 5a gives a very similar prophecy.

In summary, the lexical study shows that healing in the Old Testament era is extended to groups as well as individuals. God restored those in distress and in the process blessed them. Healing was for the heart, soul and body. While sin was the root problem that needed curing, the forgiveness of sin normally precipitated physical healing. This healing applied to broken bodies, broken spirits, broken hearts, even broken altars, dwellings and cities. Healing is also a restoration or returning to a right state. God's action of restoring a body is fourfold. He restores by 1) bringing back, 2) filling or bringing up, 3) raising and 4) infusing or putting life into. Restoration to health is the work of God even when medical means are used and the victim of illness is given the best of nursing care. Healing happens through renewal.

36

To be renewed is to be repaired, to start over, to sprout new life.

While the above are facets of biblical healing, the goal of healing is to bring man to a state of *shalom*. God desires peaceful fellowship with His children. This is best facilitated while they are experiencing *shalom*. *Shalom* meant health, fertility, longevity, prosperity and peace; this connotated completeness and security. These were all promised by God in the covenant blessing and were thus the natural consequences of remaining in the covenant. The entire context of God's Old Testament blessing and security is summed up in Psalm 128:5-6:

> May the LORD bless you from Zion
> all the days of your life:
> may you see the prosperity of Jerusalem,
> and may you live to see your
> children's children.
> Peace be upon Israel.

This was *shalom*. The Hebrew concept of *shalom* should not be compared to the popular "health and wealth" gospel of modern times. *Shalom* does mean that health or healing are part of man's total well-being. It cannot be inferred that having *shalom* means possessing the material benefits that some people today feel are necessary.

The promises, the commands, the prophecies, the instructions regarding divine healing in the Old Testament reveal four basic principles of healing: 1) Jehovah is the Healer, 2) healing is reserved for those in covenant relationship to Him, 3) healing is claimed by believing prayer and 4) healing is secured by the blood atonement. These principles are more fully developed in the New Testament by the accounts of Christ's healing ministry and the healing ministry of the early church. The epistles, though briefly, address the theology and practice of healing. What God unveils in the Old Testament of His healing grace is only a foreshadow of the splendor of healing revealed in Christ's earthly ministry and His redemptive work.

Endnotes

1. Wehham, Gordon J., *The Book of Leviticus* (Grand Rapids, MI: Eerdmans, 1979), 23-24.

2. Keith M. Bailey, *Divine Healings: The Children's Bread* (Harrisburg, PA: Christian Publications, Inc., 1977), 67.

3. Ibid., 84.

4. Peter C. Craigie, *The Book of Deuteronomy*, N.I.C.O.T. R.K. Harrison, ed. (Grand Rapids, MI: Eerdman's, 1976), 341.

5. Bailey, 70.

6. George Arthur Buttrick, ed. *The Interpreter's Dictionary of the Bible* (Nashville, TN: Abingdon Press, 1962), s.v. "Healing, Health," by R.K. Harrison, 546.

7. Ibid., 542.

8. Ibid., 546.

9. O.J. Smith, *The Great Physician* (New York: Christian Alliance Publishing, 1927), 30.

10. Ibid., 31.

11. Bailey, 95.

12. J.H. Oerter, *Divine Healing in the Light of Scriptures* (Brooklyn: Christian Alliance Publishing, 1900), 35. In this quote I have inserted the name "Yahweh" in place of "Jehovah."

13. Leslie C. Allen, *Psalms 101-150*, "Word Biblical Commentary," vol. 21 (Waco, TX: Word, 1983), 22.

14. Bailey, 78.

15. Edward J. Young, *The Book of Isaiah*, vol. III, N.I.C.O.T. R.K. Harrison, ed. (Grand Rapids, MI: Eerdmans, 1972), 345.

16. Ibid., 346.

17. T.J. McCrossan, *Bodily Healing and the Atonement* (Seattle, WA: T.J. McCrossan, 1930), 20; reprint, Tulsa OK: Faith Library, 1982.

18. A.B. Simpson, *The Gospel of Healing* (Camp Hill, PA: Christian Publications, Inc., 1986), 23.

19. A.B. Simpson, *The Lord for the Body* (Harrisburg, PA: Christian Publications, Inc., 1959), 82.

20. Ibid., 81.

21. H.C. Leupold, *Exposition of Genesis, Vol. 2* (Grand Rapids, MI: Baker Book House, 1942),

78; quoted in Keith M. Bailey, *Divine Healings: The Children's Bread* (Harrisburg, PA: Christian Publications, 1977), 64.

Chapter 2

Healing in the Time of Jesus

The God of the Bible is unchanging; His healing hand in the Old Testament is also extended in the New Testament. The Gospels and Acts detail the healing ministry of Christ and His followers. The four Gospels record 41 separate healing incidents demonstrating Jesus' divine authority and power.

An impressive amount of the gospel narrative is devoted to healing. "Of the 1,257 narrative verses in the Gospels, 484 verses—38.5 percent!—are devoted to describing Jesus' healing miracles."[1] If one adds the verses that include the immediate reactions of the crowd, the percentage of these healing-related verses exceeds 40 percent.

It is evident that the evangelists regarded healing as indispensable to the mission of Christ. They tell of Jesus either healing the sick or teaching a lesson through healing. Often Jesus preached after He had the attention of the crowd following a healing. They reported extensive details that revealed both Jesus' human and divine nature. The healings bear witness to His power, His authority and His gentle heart that understood human emotions.

Even the apostle John, who devotes the least amount of his gospel to physical healing, maintains healing as a priority.[2] Healing was an important element in Jesus' mission of redemption. Therefore, healing in the New Testament must be viewed in light of redemption. As Michael Harper asserts:

> Supremely the New Testament is about redemption or deliverance. It tells the story of how God sent his own Son on a mission of restoration, to make good the damage done since man's fall from grace.[3]

Jesus ministered from town to town where His healings, signs, wonders and powerful preaching attracted large audiences; to these audiences Jesus taught, through word and deed, the good news of redemption. The lesson was all-encompassing, for in Hebrew thinking, to be healed was to be forgiven. And forgiveness before God meant spiritual restoration.

A classic example is the healing of the paralytic let down through the roof (Matthew 9:2-8, Mark 2:3-12 and Luke 5:18-26). Jesus was in a house that was completely full. The power of the Lord was present to heal the sick (Luke 5:17). Some men brought a paralyzed friend to be healed, but there was no way to enter the building or get through the crowd to reach Jesus. The men were so determined they hauled their friend with his mat up on the roof and dug a hole through it (Mark 2:4)! This was an extremely assertive move. Think of it: Jesus, God in the flesh, is inside the house. The Spirit is moving and people are being healed. All were marveling at the sheer power of this man's therapeutic touch, when these men show up and punch a hole in the house! Would they be commended for their determination or rebuked as vandals? Perhaps even arrested?

Maybe the Pharisees would have arrested them, but Jesus sensed their faith in His power and declared the man forgiven. At this, the Pharisees were filled with contempt. And though they had not said a word, Jesus knew they hotly objected to His indirect claim of deity. His rhetorical question, "Which is easier: to say, 'Your sins are forgiven,' or to say, 'Get up and walk'?" (Luke 5:23) has no answer because neither is easier nor more difficult for the Son of God. Of course the Pharisees weren't sure of who He was yet. Looking straight at the Pharisees, He declared why He was about to perform this healing—that they may know that He had authority on earth to forgive sins. Then, in the same breath, He turned to the paralytic and told him, "Get up, take your mat and go home" (Luke 5:24b).

By simultaneously granting forgiveness of sin and physical restoration, Jesus sent a definitive message that echoes throughout the remainder of His ministry. He healed in order to confirm His authority to forgive sins. If He could so easily heal and forgive, does this not imply that He was the *source* of both? At this point, the crowd wasn't sure; they just stood there in awe.

The Nature of Healing

Healing is an essential part of the nature of Jesus. Healing, being an extension of God's character, is also an extension of Jesus' character. In his book, *The Healings of Jesus*, Michael Harper explains that the time of Jesus' ministry was to be a time of healing. This is God's plan because God is Healer. Therefore, when Jesus extended His hand of healing, He was acting out of His compassionate character toward those who were hurting. It was God in the flesh giving people a new lease on life by restoring them in body and spirit—by the thousands!

The Gospel shows that Jesus was more than a healer. He was and is the ultimate source of healing. With simplicity and quiet confidence, He healed people as easily as He breathed the air. Jesus did not strain to conjure up healing power.

People flocked to Him for healing in the same way thirsty people flock to a cool spring in the heat of summer. Sometimes when Jesus was in a crowd of people, they needed only to touch Him and they were healed (Mark 6:56). At those times one needed only to draw near and receive. Luke mentions four such incidents of unusual power for healing in his gospel (Luke 4:14, 5:17, 8:46 and 9:1-2). The account in Luke 8:46, where the woman was healed of chronic bleeding by touching the hem of Jesus' garment, is the best known of these incidents. Without making herself known to Jesus, she touched His garment and was immediately healed.

Jesus' healing power was inexhaustible. He never ran on empty. There was no need for Him to use some technique in order to gain more power. He had power. He was power. Keith Bailey says, "No limitations were placed on His healing ministry on earth."[4] To affirm the immensity of Jesus' healing power the synoptic writers give roughly 10 references to Jesus healing great multitudes. (See Appendix II, Numbers 3, 4, 8, 13, 23, 25, 27, 28 and 36 on the chart.) These crowds may have varied from 500 to 20,000 or more. The size of the crowd never taxed or weakened His power to heal. For brevity, the Gospels describe these scenes in three verses or less, simply mentioning that Jesus cured "multitudes" of people. Some have fathomed that there were even days when Jesus healed tens of thousands.

Jesus' healing was not only bountiful—it was free. Jesus liberally granted healing to anyone who would come to Him. He did not lecture people to diet or caution them as to what would have prevented their condition. He did not harangue, belittle or bill them for His services. (The price of healing today can have a way of transferring agony from the body to the wallet!) Not so with Jesus. When Jesus freed people from their anguish they were totally set free to live again.

Jesus' healings were a liberation. This liberation was symbolic of the imminent salvation through the resurrected Christ. While speaking in the local synagogue, Jesus identified Himself as the Messiah. He referred His audience to Israel's prophecy of the Spirit's authority on His ministry.

> The Spirit of the Sovereign LORD is on me,
>   because the LORD has anointed me
>   to preach good news to the poor.
> He has sent me to bind up the
>   brokenhearted
>   to proclaim freedom for the captives
>   and release from darkness for the
>   prisoners,
> to proclaim the year of the LORD's favor.
>   (Isaiah 61:1-2)

Jesus' inauguration message made clear that He had come to liberate those bound in spirit and body (Isaiah 42:7, 49:8-9, 58:6; Psalm 102:20 and 103:6).

The liberation of people from illness, sin, destruction and hell was the major theme of Jesus' work. He came to liberate people from oppression, blindness, pain, ostracism and demonization. "This is precisely how Jesus conceived His mission: the time of the Messiah would be a time of healing, of liberation, of salvation."[5] The cross made ultimate liberation irreversible. In actuality, Jesus entered the huge sin-prison called earth and walked the corridors to unlock each cell.

To disclose the reality of liberation Jesus healed the sick. (Remember, for the Hebrew, to be set free in body was to be set free indeed!) Though healing was not in itself absolute liberation, healing did proclaim liberation. Man was again free to be what he was originally intended to be: fully alive and living in joyful communion with God. For being set free is good news. McNutt says that to deny healing is to change the gospel from "Good News into Good Advice which lacks the power to transform man into a new creation."[6]

The Gospels clearly show that Jesus liberated people from demonic oppression. Twelve different examples of Jesus' healing people from insanity and demon possession are found in the Gospels (see Appendix II, Numbers 1, 3, 4, 8, 9, 14, 17, 21, 22, 31, 32 and 37). Thus liberation meant freedom from depression, emotional and mental chaos, hopelessness and grief. Harper states: "The New Testament shows us how Jesus liberated men and women from all that oppressed them. It was especially seen in terms of freedom from sickness [and] satanic powers."[7] Those who reached out to Jesus were healed and freed to fully live again.

Luke used the Greek verb *sozo* for both healing and salvation. The fact that this word is used interchangeably indicates divine healing is a redemptive act of God. Luke uses *sozo* eight times. In 6:9 it refers to "saving life"; in 8:36, releasing a demoniac; in 8:48, halting of chronic bleeding; in 8:50, returning life to a dead girl; in 17:19, the cleansing of lepers; in 23:35, 37, 39 it depicts "rescue" by those taunting

Jesus to save Himself. Some may separate the healing and saving process, but in Jesus' day they were not separate. From Luke's usage of *sozo* it can be further learned that the two processes are not supposed to be separated. In *Health and Healing*, John Wilkinson speaks with insight about the usage of this word *sozo*:

> It is clear that its wide application in the Gospels indicates that the Christian concept of healing and the Christian concept of salvation overlap to a degree which varies in different situations, but are never completely separable. Healing of the body is never purely physical, and the salvation of the soul is never purely spiritual, but both are combined in the deliverance of the whole man, a deliverance which is foreshadowed and illustrated in the healing miracles of Jesus in the Gospels.[8]

Though not coequal, healing and salvation cannot be detached from each other. For both are elements of liberation. Therefore to be physically healed by Jesus is symbolic of the coming salvation through the resurrected Christ.

By healing, Jesus manifested God's love for humanity. Undoubtedly, it is Calvary that proves the depth of His love. Healing is an overflow of Calvary's love. "The one thing that God seems to want to show people by these healings is that he is real, that he loves ordinary people, and that he wants them to draw near to him."[9] God is love; therefore His nature is love. Because He is love He heals not only out of His power but His compassion. Divine healing demonstrates what God wishes to do for all His children: give them relief, rest, peace and life. Jesus, the Son of God, worked on behalf of God and therefore functioned as the Healer, thereby relaying the message of love perfectly.

CHRISTOLOGICAL PATTERN OF HEALING

A pattern of ministry emerges from the study of Jesus' healings. There are four questions that can be raised about His mission to heal. Why did Jesus heal? What did He heal? How did He heal? How much did He heal?

Why Jesus Healed

In searching the Scriptures, I found six reasons why Jesus healed the sick. While this is not the last word on Jesus' motive and compulsion for healing, it does cover the most prominent reasons for His action.

1. As the Son of God

Jesus healed, some believe, because He was the Son of God. "Bible scholars seem to take a common position that healing was exclusively a credential of deity—a validation that Jesus was the very Son of God."[10] Jesus' healings constituted a proof of His deity. The evangelists, having realized the effect of healing, stressed it in the Gospels. Throughout biblical history (the Old Testament) God healed His children. It can only follow that Jesus would heal as God His Father had healed.

2. As Servant of the Father

Jesus healed as an act of obedience. Jesus was not a man on a glory crusade, but a man commissioned by His Father and in subjection to Him. Jesus knew that His role was that of a servant. He understood that He had been sent on a mission of love to the needy.

> The Spirit of the Lord is on me,
> because he has anointed me . . .
> He has sent me to proclaim freedom . . .
> and recovery of sight for the blind . . .
> (Luke 4:18)

Jesus clearly shows Himself as anointed and sent. So when Jesus helped man in his need, He served God. And "in taking up the cause of the helpless Jesus proves himself to be the Servant of God."[11]

After healing the man at Bethesda in John 5, Jesus gave an explanation of His work. In verse 30 He claims, "By myself I can do nothing; . . . for I seek not to please myself but him who sent me." Jesus did not accept glory for His work. His job was to bring glory to His Father who sent Him.

3. As the Prophet of God

Healing was another confirmation that Jesus

was a prophet. Though the Pharisees had been taught by the Torah that prophets were to be tested by the integrity of their prophecies, with certain people healing did add to the import of their prophetic ministry. While some of the greatest prophets did no miracles, Elijah and Elisha, still not setting the standard for what a prophet should do, were in fact unusual in their exercise of supernatural powers. So too were the prophet Jesus' works of healing.

The healings of Christ were a fulfillment of prophecy. In Matthew 8:16-17, Jesus healed every demon-possessed and sick person brought to Him. The evangelist explains, "This was to fulfill what was spoken through the prophet Isaiah: 'He took up our infirmities and carried our diseases' " (8:17).

His healings are also a fulfillment of Isaiah 61:1, which He quoted in Nazareth. Israel had been waiting since the time of Moses for the prophet who would be Messiah. Healing was one confirmation that Jesus was that prophet. The people of His day were fairly certain of what a prophet should be. Their heritage was built upon powerful men of God who did divine acts and miracles.

Though some of the greatest prophets of Israel did no miracles, Stronstad traces the prophetic similarities of Elijah, Elisha and Jesus.[12]

	ELIJAH	ELISHA	JESUS
Control	1 Kings 17:1	2 Kings 2:14	Luke 8:2ff
Nature	2 Kings 2:8	2 Kings 2:19ff	

Raise the Dead	1 Kings 17:17ff	2 Kings 4:34ff	Luke 7:14ff
Multiply Food	1 Kings 17:16 2 Kings 4:42ff	2 Kings 4:3ff	Luke 9:12ff
Heal Leprosy	2 Kings 5:8ff		Luke 5:12f f

Jesus was given great credence through His performing the same type of miracles that Elijah and Elisha had done. (Notice that the bystanders at Calvary think Jesus is calling out to Elijah: Matthew 27:47, Mark 15:35.)

There are prophetic reasons that Jesus healed in addition to fulfillment of prophecy and confirmation of His message. From a social standpoint, healing advanced Jesus' mission of restoration and redemption. For one, it feverishly spread the news about Him to people everywhere. The Gospels say that people remained for hours marveling over His mighty deeds. This gave tremendous credibility to this preaching. Healing was like an alluring flame, drawing people to Christ's ministry.

His healings, resurrections, miraculous feedings and other wonders always drew a massive crowd to hear Him preach. The whole scenario added tremendous force to His prophetic preaching about the kingdom. Consequently, Jesus continued healing until His final days.

4. Because of His Compassion

Jesus healed people because He loved and cared for them. The Scriptures record six different times when He was moved with compassion to relieve the suffering and grieving all around Him. In Appendix II, the "Healing in the Time of Jesus" chart, these are numbers 5, 18, 24, 26, 30 and 41. This compassion is the overflow of His heart.

Compassion drove Him to heal pathetic lepers eaten up with diseases. Jesus was so deeply pained at the sight of the blind that He healed them. Crowds of people with ailments often filled Him with pity. The death of Lazarus and his family's sorrow drove Jesus to tears of grief. The popular verse "Jesus wept" means Jesus sobbed as He felt the pain of Lazarus' relatives. Bailey calls Jesus' acts of compassion "an index to the very heart of God."[13]

In Walter Bauer's *Greek-English Lexicon*, "compassion" is defined "have pity; feel sympathy with or for someone in a literal and inward way; have one's heart go out to another; have compassion for someone."[14] Jesus' compassion to heal is a testimony to the tenderness and reality of the human element combined with His divine nature.

Among all the reasons Jesus healed, it is Jesus' compassion that puts Him among the crowd as one "who is touched by the feelings of infirmity." This becomes a necessary witness to who Jesus was. It intensifies the fullness of his humanity.

The verses about Jesus' compassion describe the warmth of His personality. They illustrate that He is on people who need the relief found in a divine yet human touch. His hands were warm and gentle. His eyes reflected His compassion for those in grief. His compassion attested to His love and perfect awareness of human frailty.

> This evidence . . . of mercy indicates that the healing ministry of Christ cannot be treated solely as proof of deity or of the supernatural. It must be treated also as an expression of the mercy, compassion and goodness of His pure and perfect heart.[15]

Without compassion Jesus would not have shown the meaning of true human kindness.

5. To Advance the Kingdom of God

Jesus preached and healed the sick to announce the kingdom of God. Jesus encountered the Destroyer and loosed his captives. People were being rescued from the kingdom of sin, sickness and death. The gates of hell were assaulted; its code cracked by Christ, and the oppressed were set free. In doing this, "Jesus embodied the Kingdom of God."[16] His healing ministry advanced the kingdom of God.

There are numerous references to the kingdom of God in the synoptic gospels. Scottish scholar I. Howard Marshall lists 36 in Matthew, 14 in Mark and 32 in Luke.[17] Jesus referred to the kingdom of God regularly in His preaching. Many of His sermons begin with, "The kingdom of heaven is. . . ." It was among the most important topics of His mission.

Jesus delegated His followers to proclaim the kingdom. In Luke 9:1ff and 10:1ff He sends out 12 then 72 disciples to heal and deliver people from demonization. When the 72 return from their healing and deliverance campaigns, they were thrilled that people had been healed and they said, "even the demons submit to us in your name" (Luke 10:17). Jesus responds, "I saw Satan fall like lightning from heaven." He then tells His disciples, "I have given you authority . . . to overcome all the power of the enemy." The authority over the enemy meant the presence of the kingdom of God.

The parallel saying in Matthew 12:22-30 and Luke 11:14-23 helps us understand Jesus' deliverance and healing as signs of the kingdom of God. Here Jesus' authority to heal is being challenged by religious leaders. After Jesus asserts that Satan has no part of Him, He retorts, "[I]f I drive out demons by the Spirit (Luke has "finger") of God, then the kingdom of God has come upon you" (Matthew 12:28). Jesus claimed that exorcisms announced the presence of the kingdom of God. Though the kingdom of God has always been eternal (it did not commence at some point), it was now being manifested on earth. Peter, in Acts 10:38b, says "Jesus of Nazareth . . . went around doing good and healing all who were under the power of the devil." Whereas Satan imprisons and debilitates in his kingdom, Jesus liberates and heals in His kingdom.

Jesus and Satan had two opposing agendas. Jesus offered a new creation and life while Satan offered only destruction and death. During the time of Christ's ministry, this battle between these powers raged in view of the people. This was part of the attraction of Jesus' ministry. They could actually witness the power of God winning out over evil.

6. To Defeat Satan

The winning of a war requires several processes. First, enemy territory must be reached and penetrated. Then enemy troops must be defeated and driven back as territory is reclaimed. Prisoners need to be freed and brought home. Lastly the enemy leader must be seized and a rightful rule reinstated over the land.

A parallel to war and victory can be seen in the incarnation, the ministry, the death and the resurrection of Jesus. His healings and deliverances were battles won in the war to defeat Satan. Jesus was triumphant in each of these battles. Through healing Christ reclaimed territory that had been captured by Satan in individual lives. Satan continues to harass man as he has for millenniums. Adam and Eve did not realize the immensity of the nightmare that lay ahead for all humanity as they yielded to the serpent. Man's spiritual, mental, social and physical harmony was disrupted. Jesus had come to confront the condition of human hopelessness and free men from the dominion of Satan. When Jesus healed or delivered someone, it was a direct assault on Satan's kingdom.

Since Lucifer's rebellion, his agenda has been contrary to God's. Jesus' first temptation serves as a reminder to the dissension. Here Satan offers Jesus the kingdoms of the world; Matthew 4:8-10, Luke 4:5-8. How does Jesus proceed? He rejects Satan's offer and embarks on His own mission to advance the kingdom of God. His method would be to set people free from the kingdom of Satan and build His Church against which nothing would prevail against. First John 3:8b says. "[T]he devil has been sinning from the beginning. The reason the Son of God appeared was to destroy the devil's work." That is why healing is a large part of Jesus' work. Though not every sickness is a satanic work, healing is a weapon that counterattacks Satan.

Satan's empire is one ultimately bent on inflicting agony. Being diametrically opposed to God, Satan's attacks are upon creation and man. Satan effected a break in man's relationship with the Creator. The wicked environment Satan has designed is hostile to God and miserable for man. As if this were not enough, Satan sent demons to actually occupy individuals and ruin their lives. This was his foretaste of hell.

Into this scene of wretchedness came the Prince of Peace to proclaim the Good News of the kingdom and to demonstrate the power of the kingdom by casting out demons, healing sickness, disease, deformities, handicaps and raising the dead. Jesus had executed a powerful work. Satan's losses were real and limited authority on earth.

Jesus invaded Satan's empire counterattacking by forgiveness, healing and exorcism. Jesus dealt with sin and sickness with precision, power and authority as it had never been dealt with before. He knew that the origin of sickness was rooted in the Deceiver. "In the New Testament, sickness is seen as an extension and effect of sin and . . . therefore evil in origin."[18] Everything about Christ's life and ministry confronted and defeated Satan.

What Jesus Healed

The healing ministry of Jesus Christ was very comprehensive and covered the whole spectrum of human needs.

1. Sickness, Disease, Deformity, Handicap, Death

Jesus demonstrated His power and authority to heal a wide variety of sicknesses, diseases, deformities, handicaps and spiritual disorders. The record of His physical healings in the Gospels may be arranged in five categories: internal diseases, chronic diseases, sensory diseases, deformities and various assorted problems.

Internal Diseases
fevers
sickness (mild or deadly)
hemorrhaging
dropsy or edema (excessive fluid in the tissues)
"severe pain"

Chronic Diseases
man lame 38 years
leprosy

hemorrhaging (12 years)
(these last two diseases required that the victims
be in isolation)

Sensory Diseases
blindness
deafness
mute/dumb
leprosy (it affected "touch")

Deformities
withered hand
crippled, lame
paralysis
scoliosis/bent spine

Assorted Problems
severed body parts (ear)
neurological disorders and
epilepsy
demonization
death or the critically ill
various/all diseases

The list above is certainly not inclusive of every disease that existed in Jesus' day. However, the healing by Jesus recorded in the Gospels is a clear statement of Jesus' complete mastery over all human ailments.

2. Sin and Spiritual Sickness

The biblical record clearly teaches that the

spiritual sickness of sin lies at the root of all human problems. Stated plainly, Jesus came to remedy the sin problem. "Every time Jesus met with evil, spiritual or physical, he treated it as an enemy."[19] He did so because evil is sin and sin is lethal. Sin and its effects never puzzled Jesus because He knew its origin. He knew the grave effects of spiritual sickness. "Spiritual sickness . . . disrupts our emotions, our relationships and even our physical bodies."[20] At times, Jesus would treat the sin and the physical symptom would be healed as in the case of the paralytic referred to earlier, the one lowered through the roof (Matthew 9:1-8; Mark 2:1-12; Luke 5:17-26). Upon seeing their faith (both Mark and Luke's first usage of the word "faith") Jesus said to the man, "[Y]our sins are forgiven" (Matthew 9:2). He could have merely repaired the man's defective body parts but it was time to expose the core of human malady and also His own authority to remedy that condition.

The truth that healing and forgiveness are related was not new; God had revealed it in the Old Testament. The people were astounded when Jesus spoke forgiveness. It was harder for them to believe Jesus could forgive than it was to believe He could heal. They did not yet understand that He was God. This incident of the paralytic tells of the extent and fullness of Jesus' power and authority over sin.

Note where this healing had fallen in the progression of Jesus' healing ministry. Up until this point, Luke has testified to the breadth of Jesus' miraculous power as one who had performed exorcisms, 4:35 and 41; cured a fever, 4:39; healed "various diseases," 4:40; exhibited control over nature, 5:4-7; and cleansed a leper, 5:13. By this, Luke establishes the fact that Jesus is extraordinary before telling the story of the paralytic. In this second reference to "power" being upon Jesus, it was now time to reveal the extent of His power . . . His authority to forgive sin.

Matthew, Mark and Luke place this healing near the beginning of their narratives so that the subsequent healings can be read in light of this revelation. Thus, sin and sickness are linked—and Jesus solves both problems. After Jesus declared the man to be forgiven, the angry Pharisees retorted, "Who can forgive sins but God alone?" Jesus cut to the issue by asking, "Which is easier: to say, 'Your sins are forgiven,' or to say, 'Get up and walk'?" (Luke 5:23). The answer is that neither is easier to say. Neither is easier to say because neither is harder to do.

Joseph Fitzmyer says, "The physical miracle is the sign of the rescue of the man from the bonds of moral evil."[21] Once these bonds were loosed by forgiveness, the paralysis was healed and he rose from his mat. Being forgiven and healed, his life was now returned to wholeness. "It suggests the extraordinary character of the new dimension in human life that comes with Jesus' power and authority."[22] The lesson was that Jesus can both heal and forgive, and people ought to go to Him for both blessings.

3. *Demonization*

Jesus freed those who were bound by demons. The Gospels record Jesus casting out demons on 11 different occasions. These accounts are important, for they illustrate Jesus' authority and power to overcome the evil one. They also offer people a message of hope through Christ for power to free them from fear of the demons. Demons have one assignment, and that is to work destruction in human personalities. If given free reign, they would do so.

The following list covers the characteristics of demons:

> They have intelligence (Acts 16:16-18; 19:15-16).
> They are spirits (Matthew 8:16; 12:43-45; Luke 10:17-20; Revelation 16:14).
> They manifest themselves in different forms (Revelation 9:1-12; 16:13-14).
> They are malevolent (Matthew 12:43-45; Mark 1:27; 3:11; Luke 4:36; Acts 8:7; Revelation 16:13).
> They know their own end (Matthew 8:29; 25:41; James 2:19).
> They have supernatural strength (Matthew 12:29; Mark 5:4; Luke 8:29; Acts 19:13-16).
> They must bow to Jesus' name (Matthew 8:28-34; Mark 5:7; Luke 8:26-33).[23]

In their never-ending attempt to invade human beings, the demons will initially attack through the mind. If they did not they would be too easily exposed as workers of evil. Their strategy is to spiritually assault the mind and manipulate people physically so that it looks as if the problem is self-inflicted. In this way the devil keeps people preoccupied with the symptoms of his work which can in turn divert them from dealing with the root. Jesus recognized demonization when He saw it. He would quickly expel the "demons at work" as well as reverse the destruction they had caused.

For example, the most ostentatious display of demonization was in the Gerasene demoniac (Matthew 8:28, Mark 5:1-20, Luke 8:26-39). Fitzmyer calls it "fantastic" and "grotesque."[24] The man had been reduced to a worse than animal state. Jesus met him to administer healing and peace and to display authority and power over the demons. This deliverance occurred directly after the storm on Galilee as described in all three Synoptics. "The Jesus who stilled the storm on the lake, and took authority over the elements, also took authority over the storm in this man's life."[25]

The satanic team was hard at work in this man. He made the whole area a threat to pass through. He wore no clothes and, obsessed with death, he lived among the tombs. With satanic strength he broke every chain they put him in. He did not sleep. Day and night he roamed the hills crying out and cutting himself. His life had been reduced to a maniacal nightmare.

When Jesus arrived, a power encounter took place. The man was delivered. The demons entered the herd of pigs who then rushed down the cliff to their death. When the city dwellers heard about this they came to see what had happened. "When they came to Jesus, they found the man from whom the demons had gone out, sitting at Jesus' feet, dressed and in his right mind" (Luke 8:35). He had been brought back from his demented state to wholeness. This marvelous display of Jesus' power and authority was a great victory.

The point to be remembered from the deliverance of the Gerasene demoniac and the other healings is that Jesus has the power and authority to heal anything Satan may inflict. No matter what level of demonization victims suffer Jesus can make them whole. Jesus' healing reverses the work of demons and expels them so that those left in their hideous wake may return to a sane, productive, joyful life.

How Jesus Healed

There were two important factors in how Jesus carried out His healing ministry. First, Jesus was empowered by the Holy Spirit of God for this ministry. Second, Jesus required faith from those who desired healing.

1. Through the Anointing of the Spirit of God

Jesus delivered and healed people through the power of the Holy Spirit. Any conflicting belief is heresy. He was God in the flesh and was capable of doing any of these works in His own power.

But for the purpose of His incarnation, Jesus laid aside His power and carried out His ministry as a man filled with the Holy Spirit (Luke 4:18-19). Prior to Jesus' baptism there is no record of Him performing any miracles. The only remarkable event during His first 30 years is the Temple incident when He was 12 years old. Here He displays precocious knowledge about Yahweh and related matters. Any other details about supernatural works are sensational exploits, ill-founded at best.

Jesus' deeds are acts of the Spirit. They are not initiated independently. Of the four evangelists, Luke illustrates this the most clearly. For him, the activity of the Holy Spirit is perfectly lived out in the ministry of Jesus. There is not a hint of ego operating in Jesus either by word or gesture while He is healing. He is fueled by the Holy Spirit, fully human and fully God. Since Jesus' ministry is ordained of God, it is, in essence, His call. Therefore "the gift of the Spirit to Jesus in the inauguration narrative . . . is vocational. This vocational gift is specifically prophetic. Jesus is not only anointed by the Spirit, but He is also Spirit-led, Spirit-filled, and Spirit-empowered."[26]

It was by the Spirit that Jesus commenced the work of the kingdom of God. It was by the Spirit that He healed the sick, blind, lame, raised the dead and preached the Good News. From His baptism to His ascension, Jesus was completely gifted for His work. Jesus labored in dependency upon the Holy Spirit throughout the length of His ministry.

2. *Through Elemental Faith*

Faith is a requirement for Christ's healing touch to be received. Norman Perrin says, "Many of the most characteristic sayings about faith in the gospels are associated with miracles, especially healing miracles."[27] It is almost as if faith is the spark that starts a fire. Faith is seen nearly to melt Jesus' heart (if such a verb is permissible). When He saw faith in a person He had a practical compulsion to heal them. The Gospel writers specifically note faith as the catalyst in at least 13 of the 41 recorded miracles. Jesus was stirred to action by faith in such incidents as the paralytic (see number 6 in Appendix II: "Jesus' Works at Healing"), with Jairus and his daughter (see number 10), the Syro-phoenician and her daughter (number 14), the blind Bartimaeus (number 18) and the centurion with his servant (number 19). Faith could be expressed on the part of the sick or by someone else who cared for them. It was of no matter. People expressed faith, for instance, by obeying Jesus' commands like "go wash in Siloam" or "stretch out your hand."

Lack of faith was the only apparent barrier to Jesus' healing ministry. When He returned to Nazareth after His baptism, His healing power was hindered by unbelief (Matthew 13:58, Mark 6:5-6). Matthew says that He "did not do," but Mark goes so far as to say He "*could* there do no mighty work" (KJV, emphasis added). These Scriptures imply a refusal to violate a theological law. Not that lack of faith nullified the omnipotence of God, but simply that He would not force them to have faith in Him. If He did, it would be like a parent begging a stubborn four-year-old to open a birthday present. This would be nonsense. God will not beg to bless anyone.

It is important to clarify this "faith" concept. Faith is not a coin for healing that will turn God into a therapeutic vending machine. The "name it, claim it" hype is excessive sensationalism. Faith is believing Jesus is able and willing to heal. Christ's followers are obligated to express faith for healing. If not, then it is Christians who say "no" to God's healing touch, not God. Only God has the prerogative to withhold healing. Some use the "if it be Your will" clause as a disguise for presuppositional unbelief.

Thus faith opens the way for people to receive healing. Faith clears the channel through which healing can flow. True faith does not demand of God, but humbly petitions with full hope of a response. True faith asks of God and eagerly awaits.

How Much Did Jesus Heal?

The title question may sound peculiar, but it deserves explanation. Did Jesus cure mental retardation? Were there no stillborn babies during His ministry? Were all the hospitals in Israel and Judah empty by the time He finished His travels? Was this His objective? Because of the final verse in John's gospel that says, "Jesus did many other things as well," dogmatic answers to such questions become difficult to make. However, the details of Jesus' ministry are ample enough to draw the following conclusions.

1. What He Did, He Did Completely

Those that Jesus healed were completely healed. This means that no one who had faith and had been healed by Jesus left His presence in need. "The evangelists never show him counseling a sick man to rejoice or to be patient because disease is helpful or redemptive. Instead Jesus cured them all (e.g. Matthew 12:15)."[28] Granted, just because perfect healing was granted to these persons, many of them did not follow Christ.

To merely counsel the sick on "how to have faith and strength despite your circumstances" would be an invalid substitute for healing. Jesus' aim was to heal them, not just to give them a positive attitude and improve their mental outlook.

The healing that Christ administered was precise and perfect. He did not overlook the pain of any person. No one left Him to see a "specialist" for a second opinion. Jesus in man equals man put back together again—in other words, returned to harmony. Through the incarnation:

> . . . there is a new quality of life which is now given to men and women through the life and death of Jesus Christ. . . . It has myriads of features, each of which sparkles with its own iridescence. The health which Christ brings is never dull or stereotyped.[29]

Jesus' authority to heal was omnipotent in terms of quantity as well as quality. In several places the Gospels say, "He . . . healed all that were sick." In other places it says, "As many as touched him were made whole."[30] Jesus would heal a multitude as easily and perfectly as He would heal an individual.

The health that Jesus bestowed brings tremendous joy. Healing now is but a small foretaste of the health, liberation and joyful fellowship with God that man will have in the kingdom that is yet to come in all its fullness.

At the same time, there are some things that "complete healing in Jesus" does *not* mean. For one, it is not a "cosmic Christian health" theory, as if once healed by Jesus one can expect to be in an enduring state of A-1 health. Complete healing does not mean permanent perfection. Those who were healed by Jesus did not feel like 19 years old when they were 91. This would be promoting youth, making Jesus the fountain of youth. God's objective in healing extends far beyond physical health.

Neither does divine healing embody nor promote the "health and wealth" heresy. The healings were for a higher purpose. They are not an end in themselves but a call to repentance, salvation, holiness and commitment to God. Jesus healed man to glorify God, not promote man.

"Complete healing" was not a Hebrew health care plan. Jesus' presence in Israel and Judah did not mean that leprosy was eliminated, everyone had 20/20 vision and morticians lost all business. Subsequently, neither did the Church become the "flawless club," where everyone in every pew had two percent body fat. Such caricatures are the embellishments of Greek mythology and wishful nonthinking "charismaniacs," not Judeo-Christian theology. All those that Jesus healed in Israel eventually aged and died like all others. For even though He gave complete healing, death is a post-Eden passage that cannot be escaped.

2. Healing in the Light of His Coming Kingdom

It may seem a puzzle that, with Jesus as the manifest solution to man's plight, even after His ministry in the Spirit and His granting the fullness of the Spirit, that odious problems—including sickness and death—still persist. The answer to this puzzle is having a proper understanding of the kingdom of God. Jesus announced the kingdom and predicted its future manifestation.

Jesus' ministry commenced the kingdom of God. It was like a starting gun at the beginning of a race. The race is not yet over, but Jesus' lead is insurmountable. Likewise, with God's hand at work there is much happening now, but there is much that is still unfulfilled of kingdom blessing. Final victory will be at the finish line. God is not finished.

Granted, healing takes place as God moves and faith invites. But consummate healing will be at the rapture. During this present era in history the bride of Christ, the Church, is engaged to be perfectly restored unto God her creator. Then, in that day, God will permanently heal *all* who are His own in *every* way. But not before the day of His return. Until then Christ's power is manifestly here, internalized in the Church.

In time, Jesus will fully manifest Himself in the kingdom of God. It will be a dominion where there is neither sickness, sorrow, hunger nor death. Jesus did not obliterate these problems for it was not yet time to. He offered healing and triumph within life's problems. This is how Jesus launched the initial assault on the kingdom of darkness. It was a precursor to what He will do completely in the fullness of time. He asserted the kingdom of God by His ministry and message which included healing. This was God's way of offering a foretaste of eternity.

The healing hand of Jesus is at work just the same. And believers ought to pray and not give up, for the promise of complete healing still stands. The matter of "when" is in God's hands. God controls His children, not vice versa. All God's own will be healed completely, when Christ returns. Yet, as the Gospels clearly illustrate, some are totally healed sooner. In fact, one of Jesus' commissions to His disciples was to heal the sick.

Endnotes

1. John Wimber, *Power Healing* (San Francisco: Harper & Row, 1987), 41.

2. John includes four healings of individuals and one multitude healing. But these five events are comprehensive and assert that Jesus is the authoritative Healer. John 4 and 5 have adjacent healings. In John 4 He heals the official's son at a distance. In John 5 the 38-year paralytic is healed. Note that these two healings did not take place together but John puts them together (see John 5:1) to prove that whether one is prestigious, wealthy, grieving and near death or poor, banished, chronically ill and depressed, Jesus can heal you. In John 6 the great crowd He would soon feed is impressed with His healing power. John 9 is devoted to the healing of the man born blind and interpreting that miracle as simply for the glory of God. In John 11, Jesus displays His mastery over death by resurrecting Lazarus. So even John, in his five healings, declares that the healings are pivotal for confirming that Jesus is the Savior.

3. Michael Harper, *The Healings of Jesus*, The Jesus Library, ed. Michael Green (Downers Grove, IL: InterVarsity Press, 1986), 147.

4. Keith Bailey, *Divine Healing: The Children's Bread* (Harrisburg, PA: Christian Publications, Inc., 1977), 101.

5. Francis MacNutt, *Healing* (Notre Dame, IN: Ave Maria Press, 1985), 52.

6. Ibid., 108.

7. Harper, 22-23.

8. Wimber, 38; quoted in John Wilkinson, *Health and Healing* (Edinburgh: Handsel, 1980), 33.

9. MacNutt, 93.

10. Bailey, 98.

11. F. Graber and D. Muller, "Heal," in *The New International Dictionary of New Testament Theology Vol. 2*, ed. Colin Brown (Grand Rapids, MI: Zondervan Publishing House, 1976), 165.

12. Roger Stronstad, *The Charismatic Theology of St. Luke* (Peabody, MA: Hendrickson Publishers, 1984), 44.

13. Bailey, 101.

14. Bauer, Arndt, Gingrich and Danker, *A Greek-English Lexicon of the New Testament* (Chicago: University of Chicago Press, 1979), 762-763.

15. Bailey, 98-99.

16. Wimber, 41.

17. I. Howard Marshall, *Luke: Historian and Theologian* (Grand Rapids, MI: Zondervan, 1970), 89.

18. Wimber, 36.

19. MacNutt, 62.

20. Wimber, 71.

21. Fitzmyer, 585.

22. Ibid., 586.

23. Wimber, 106.

24. Fitzmyer, 734.

25. Harper, 41.

26. Stronstad, 45.

27. Norman Perrin, *Rediscovering the Teaching of Jesus* (New York: Harper & Row, 1976), 131.

28. MacNutt, 79.

29. Harper, 147.

30. A.B. Simpson, *The Gospel of Healing* (Camp Hill, PA: Christian Publications, Inc., 1986), 18.

Chapter 3

Healing in the Apostolic Era

T he disciples continued Jesus' ministry of divine healing with the same power and effect
that Jesus had in His ministry. Were they acting
on their own? What was their purpose? Or were
they His servants following orders?

The Commission to Heal

Jesus did not keep the ministry of healing to
Himself, but passed it on to His followers. This
began in Matthew 10:1ff; Mark 3:13ff and Luke
9:1ff. He gave them the power and authority to
drive out all demonic forces and cure diseases, and
sent them out to preach the kingdom and to heal
the sick, Luke 9:2.

In Luke 10 Jesus commissioned 72 others to go
and do the same. They were thrilled about the results. They had demonstrated healings and deliverance from demonic power. The 72 were
ordinary disciples who had been with Jesus and
had observed His amazing authority and power.
But this time He did something they probably

had not planned on. Jesus sent *them* out with authority and power.

The Luke 9 and 10 internships had transformed these men. Up until now, they had simply witnessed Jesus casting out demons and healing. Now they realized that they could go out in Jesus' name and do these same works. They were stunned and delighted. What they didn't know yet was that Jesus was preparing them for the time they would take up the whole ministry of the gospel. Therefore, we can see that "it is clear that Jesus taught his disciples to take the same uncompromising stand toward sickness."[1] The disciples had now done it themselves; they had healed and they would never be the same. The ministry of the divine healing was to continue after Jesus departed. He had not come just to give temporary relief from the hand of the enemy. Satan had tormented humanity long enough. But Jesus had now fractured Satan's ramparts. And though Jesus was to leave shortly, His followers were to continue ministering wholeness to people.

In the "Great Commission," Matthew 28:18ff, Jesus declared His total authority and instructed them to go make disciples, baptizing them and teaching them to obey everything He had commanded them. Part of what He had commanded them was to heal the sick. Jesus demonstrated this and taught His followers to model after Him. Later, as He was preparing for His final departure, He urged them to stay in Jerusalem until the

Holy Spirit came, then go do as Jesus had done. The orders were clear.

They were told to obey all the Master's commands and preach the gospel. Their message was to be a complete gospel and not a partial gospel. Jesus came and liberated by preaching and healing. They were to "go and do likewise."[2] The disciples realized that Jesus was the perfect model for living life unto God in faith and practice. His healing ministry could not be ignored. They could do nothing less than continue in all they had learned of the power of God.

The Healing Ministry of the Disciples

The disciples' phenomenal ministry of healing was a testimony to the power of Jesus. As in Jesus' ministry, healing served to advance their message: Christ Jesus and the kingdom of God. Healing was a means to preaching, which led to conversion and baptism in the Holy Spirit. Healing also taught a powerful lesson about God's love which built up believers and further blessed the church.

In Matthew 16:19 Jesus tells Peter that he will be given the keys to the kingdom of heaven. This loaded verse foretells of Peter's ongoing ministry wherein he will be teaching, preaching the kingdom and exercising divine healing.

In the Book of Acts, Luke records many healings the apostles did. He begins with signs and wonders after the day of Pentecost. Chapter three tells of the healing of the lame beggar by Peter and John. There were numerous apostolic signs, wonders, healings and exorcisms in chapter 5. Chapters 6 and 8 respectively narrate Stephen's and Philip's powerful ministries. They performed wonders and miraculous signs, cast out demons and healed paralytics and cripples. Ananias restores sight to Saul (Paul) after his conversion. Peter renders back-to-back miracles in healing Aeneas of paralysis and raising Dorcas from the dead (9:32-43). Then Paul appears upon the scene. He and Barnabas confirm their message of grace through miraculous signs and wonders. Paul heals a lame man in Lystra, then does what Luke calls "amazing miracles," 19:11ff. In chapter 20, Paul raises Eutychus after a deadly fall. Finally, on Malta Paul survives a snakebite. He then heals Publius' father of fever and dysentery and everyone else on the island of their maladies.

The healing ministry of the apostles bears striking resemblance to Jesus' healings. There was a continuity in the work of the Holy Spirit from the ministry of Jesus that carries into the ministry of the apostles. Jesus has departed, but the same Spirit is now working through the disciples. While there is continuity, at the same time there is a discontinuity.

Jesus and the apostles both preach the kingdom of God. Both heal the sick and lame. The difference is that Jesus was declaring Himself to be the Healer and the way to reach that kingdom. The apostles have no such agenda for themselves. For example, the apostles are never heard saying anything like, "I am the truth" or "[C]ome to me all

you who are weary." They make no self-asser-
tions. Their aim is to exalt Christ alone.

The apostles did not perform nature miracles or
miraculous feedings. A healing is for a blessing; a
nature miracle is purely for display of power. For
instance, there was more shock than joy when Jesus walked on water or calmed the sea. Granted,
the healings and exorcisms were marvelous, but
their motive was to bless people and exalt Christ.
The apostles were merely chosen foot soldiers in a
movement to build Christ's Church.

Jesus said that His followers would *do* greater
things than He had done; John 14:12-14. But He
never said that they would *be* greater men. There
is a monumental difference. It should be noted
that "greater" does not mean "better." Neither
does it mean that they will do more phenomenal
things. "*Mega,*" the Greek word for "greater,"
means a different size or number and is not a reference to intrinsic value. The greater works were
accomplished through the power of the Holy
Spirit. This means that the disciples were not
their own source of power.

The Mission of the Epistles of Paul and James

The Epistles do not mention healing nearly as
much as the Gospels. This is because the Epistles
of Paul and James are written for an entirely different reason than the Gospels. By the time the
Epistles are written, many churches had been
planted; healing was already widely experienced.
Though many Christians had not yet read a copy

of the Gospels, the testimony of the gospel of Christ had been confirmed by supernatural wonders. Christians were receiving divine healing as the Church by the Holy Spirit ministered to them. Therefore it is unnecessary for Paul and James to write extensively about divine healing. It needed no further assertion for the young Church.

Paul and James wrote their Epistles to instruct people in the practical means of holy living. James reminds believers to live their faith through actions that glorify God. Paul had the delicate task of balancing the "charismania" in certain churches (Corinth in particular) without quenching the work of the Holy Spirit. Of Paul's work in Corinth, Marion Soards observes, "He refrains from displays of power, ministering in and through affliction, so that true divine power, as revealed in Jesus Christ, may work through him."[3] In short, Paul had the task of interpreting the life of Jesus for the entire Church.

Though little is said about healing in the Epistles, especially when compared to the Gospels, Paul and James certainly believed in it. James was an eyewitness to Christ's spectacular healing ministry. Paul personally experienced healing from blindness several days after his conversion (Acts 9). Probably the most astounding incident is seen in Acts 28:1-10. Paul is sitting beside a fire on Malta after being shipwrecked. A poisonous snake comes up out of the firewood and bites down on his hand. He survives the snakebite and later heals the father of the island chief. The natives were so impressed that all the sick on the entire island came for healing. Paul healed every one of them. Therefore we can be certain that both Paul and James knew about divine healing from personal experience.

Luke, in the book of Acts, describes Paul's ministry of healing. Healing was important to Paul. His view of healing never diminishes even though he makes little mention of it in his 13 letters. There is no reason to believe that he changed his belief about healing. In his letter to the Romans, Paul says, "[He] who raised Christ from the dead will also give life to your mortal bodies through his Spirit, who lives in you" (Romans 8:11).

Paul and James had the particular task of helping the young Church grow. They believed in, and practiced, divine healing as did the four evangelists Matthew, Mark, Luke and John. Paul and James simply present healing in the larger context of New Testament church life.

Paul's Perspective and Presentation of Healing

Paul, in his epistles, deals with questions that were arising among the Christians who are still young in their faith. For example, what about when someone who seems to have faith is not healed? How about Paul's own aches and pains? And why did Paul talk about healing so little?

1. Healing as One of the Gifts

Healing is a gift that a person may receive and use to build up the Body of Christ. Romans 12:6ff reads, "We have different gifts, according to the grace given us." In First Corinthians 4:7, Paul asks "What do you have that you did not receive?" Later in First Corinthians 12:4-11 he talks about different kinds of gifts that all come from the same Spirit. These are words of wisdom, words of knowledge, faith, healing, prophecy, tongues and others. In Ephesians 4, Paul says that it is Christ's Spirit who gave gifts to some to be apostles, prophets, evangelists, pastors and teachers.

All these different gifts, including healing, are diverse and are dispersed throughout the Church for edification and to benefit the Body of Christ. Here Paul is teaching the interdependence of the Body of Christ, and healing is a given. By now healing is regularly experienced in the Church. Paul assumes this and writes of his greater concern: that Christians grow in their faith and love toward each other.

Paul refers to those with the gifts of healings as practical specialists. A specific person will have a specific gift. And that person is to use his gift, healing included. Paul's teaching is similar in concept to a modern hospital. A problem with either the heart, brain or bones requires a different specialist. That specialist deals with specific problems and injuries. So too with people with the gift of healing in a church. They have a role that must be filled in obedience and the power of the Holy Spirit. They are not local folk-heroes, just Christians within the church who have a call to follow Christ.

2. Paul's View of Healing in This Age

During the earthly ministry of Christ, He frequently healed all who were sick. But after Christ's ascension, sickness persisted in Christian circles. While healing was available, not all were healed. What were the Christians then—and now—to make of this? How did Paul deal with the dilemma? Some scholars believe that Paul's eschatology (the study of "the end") offers an answer.

Scholars have come to call this theme "apocalyptic." " 'Apocalyptic' is a special expression of Jewish eschatology [the study of the end] that was characterized by the dualistic doctrine of two ages."[4] The present age is marked by the mundane, evil, drudgery and temporality. However, "the 'age to come' is the supernatural realm of the power of God."[5] The shift from this age to the age of God-rule would be distinctly marked by God's mighty intervention. The present evil age would halt and the new would begin.

The classic study of Paul's apocalyptic theory was done by Geerhardus Vos in his book, *The Pauline Eschatology*. A half century later Oscar Cullman wrote *Christ and Time* and further developed the interpretation of the apocalyptic. In 1987 Marion L. Soards wrote a treatment of Pauline eschatology in which he describes the Jewish "apocalyptic" concept as follows:

God's Intervention

V

The Present Evil Age   *The Age to Come*[6]

In the latter age glory, justice and peace would triumph. According to Soards, Paul's line of

thinking is tied into Jewish apocalyptic thought.
He maintains the two distinct ages, the evil age
and the glorious age to come. "But he modifies the
scheme in light of the Christ-event so that there
are two distinct ages that are separated and joined
by an interim."[7]

It is illustrated as:

GOD'S INTERVENTION IN:

THE CROSS OF   THE COMING OF
JESUS CHRIST   JESUS CHRIST

V   **V**

THE PRESENT   THE ENDS OF   A NEW
EVIL AGE   THE AGES   CREATION[8]

Paul saw himself as living between the two advents. Yes, Jesus Christ the Savior had come. Sin,
Satan and death had been defeated. The Law had
been lifted. Creation had been won back. But
there were more battles yet to be fought before all
would be brought to completion. This explains
the intermingling of present suffering along with
the Spirit's presence and promise of Christ's return in all His fullness and glory.

So Christians live between *and* within both the
old and the new eras. "Christ had become the
first-fruits of the new order (1 Corinthians 15:23)
but the Christian still awaits the end [of the old
order] (v. 24)."[9] Therefore the final restoration of
health will be in the end of time. Soards says,
"Christians living at the juncture of the ages await

Christ's coming at the absolute end of the present evil age."[10] Paul wrote of this concept in Philippians 3:17-21.

While the problems (the problem(s) being: why are there still sick people among us when Jesus, who is able to heal the sick, is dynamically present among us?) raised by those who believe the "Apocalyptic Theory" do have an eschatological dimension, eschatology is not the only issue in the resolution of these problems. The adherents to the above "Apocalyptic Theory" are right in their observation that final restoration of health will be at the end of time. They are also correct in their observation that sickness will continue and healing will not be complete until Christ's return. However, the following question should be asked: Why should Paul use the Jewish eschatology when he, like all the other apostles, had a new Christian eschatology given to him by revelation? The "Apocalyptic Theory" avoids both the teaching of a literal millennial reign of Christ on earth and the Old Testament prophecies of healings during the millennial reign (Isaiah 35:5-6). While the problems raised by those who believe the "Apocalyptic Theory" do have an eschatological dimension, eschatology is not the only issue in the resolution of these problems.

There are other possible explanations of the problems of continued sickness among Christians and the fact that not all are healed. A plausible answer is to distinguish two kinds of healing presented in the New Testament. The healings of

Jesus and the healings that occurred on the cutting edge of missionary advance depicted in the Acts of the Apostles were sovereign and served as confirming signs of the gospel of Christ. Such healings still occur all over the world. Those who were healed were unbelievers for the most part. In many instances they became Christians after experiencing the healing power of Christ.

Paul and James address the healing of the sick within the context of the church—the healing of Christians. Paul's teaching recognizes the healing of the Christian to be conditional. Paul says that the body of the Christian must be for the Lord and the Lord for the body (1 Corinthians 6:13). Paul calls for the purity and consecration of the believer's body. Paul, like James, saw the necessity of seeking forgiveness and correcting behavior as a prerequisite to healing (James 5:15).

James also pointed out that the lack of unity and spiritual health in the assembly would hinder healing. Unlike the sign healings, the healing of Christians entails the confession and forsaking of sin. Thus healing was sometimes delayed or denied because the individual seeking healing was not right with God or other Christians.

3. Interpreting Paul's "Thorn in the Flesh"

Paul's "thorn in the flesh" is another factor in this discussion of the continuation of sickness. In this interim period before Christ comes while the devil, though defeated, has not yet been expelled, Paul's testimony shows the menace this situation presents to Christians. The apostle's testimony in Second Corinthians 12:7-9 says:

> To keep me from becoming conceited be-
> cause of these surpassing great revelations,
> there was given me a thorn in my flesh, a
> messenger of Satan, to torment me. Three
> times I pleaded with the Lord to take it
> away from me. But he said to me, "My grace
> is sufficient for you, for my power is made
> perfect in weakness."

This passage from Paul's personal experience is important for several reasons. First, though Satan has been defeated, he does have access to us, for he has not yet been obliterated and he can directly interfere to bring grief. Second, it casts a long shadow across the idea that says "enough faith can change anything," as if the faith of God's children controlled God. Third, it is strong evidence against the idea that God needs people to be happy and healthy in order to use them. Fourth, it tells us that things are different in God's world. God sees and operates on a level essentially higher than that of humanity. Because of this He will do what He must, to accomplish what He must, even if we finite and fallen creatures object to God's processes.

The definition of the phrase "thorn in the flesh" can be difficult to pinpoint. V.P. Furnish lays out the major possibilities in three general categories: First, the "thorn in the flesh" could be an inner struggle. Perhaps it was a carnal temptation or spiritual weakness; perhaps sexual temptation. "This was a favorite view in the Middle Ages."[11] Others argue it was a sense of unworthiness, guilty conscience or agony about the Jews who would not believe. On this view, the point is that it kept him humble.

Second, the "thorn" may have been physical. Furnish says, "This is the most widely accepted view, at least in modern times."[12] Some church fathers feel it was a "headache" that Paul is talking about. Because of periodic comments made in his letters, if the "thorn " is physical, it could be a sensory problem, such as solar retinitis or a speech impediment. It is possible that Paul suffered from a malarial fever that recurred in his travels.

Lightfoot suggests epilepsy, "possibly as a result of the experience Paul had at his conversion."[13] But theories about some sort of mentally or psychosomatically rooted illness such as hysteria or depression do come under serious question. Paul's thinking is too lucid and his influence is too prevalent to be coming from someone who is periodically delirious.

Ralph P. Martin wonders whether the problem really was physical: "With all these physical ailments suggested, one wonders . . . whether or not a person who was so often on the 'battlefield,' could have been so physically weak and still have withstood the rigors of Paul's life."[14] This is a valid point, for Paul was a strong character, whose personal influence was felt throughout the Christian world. Could he have done all that he did and been so frail?

According to V.P. Furnish, the third possibility for Paul's "thorn" is that it is persecution from an exterior source, such as a person or group. Ancient Christian writers Chrysostom, Augustine and Theodoret argue this. Furnish gives five reasons for such a possibility. First, note that Paul, in Second Corinthians 11:13-15, refers to certain men who are servants of Satan. And in Second Corinthians 12:7c Paul says that this messenger of Satan was sent "to torment me (*kolaphizein*)." Second, the only other usage of this Greek word by Paul is in First Corinthians 4:11c. He is talking about brutal treatment from other humans. Third, in the Septuagint version of the Old Testament, Numbers 33:55 and Ezekiel 28:24 speak of Israel's enemies as "thorns." Fourth, " 'in the flesh' may be understood to refer to one's whole earthly existence."[15] And fifth, because of the context, Paul is talking about hardship at the hands of others before (2 Corinthians 11:23a) and after he mentions this "thorn" (2 Corinthians 12:10a).

Jerry McCant takes this third point further and argues that Paul's thorn in the flesh is *rejected apostleship*. He says, "The 'thorn in the flesh' is not a physical malady but refers to certain persons."[16] This may be why 10 of his 13 letters assert his apostleship in the greeting or subscript. Apparently some opponents do not seem to acknowledge the office Paul holds. These scoffers may be Judaizing Christians (who still required circumcision), gnostics (who claim that knowledge with certainty is unattainable), allegorizers (those who dismiss biblical stories as mere allegory not history), Jews from Palestine or some representatives of pneumatic Christology (the belief that Christ was a spirit only and not a man with a body).

After scanning the possibilities, McCant labels Corinth as Paul's problem. He claims that by using certain literative techniques, "Paul depicts Corinth as a sick church inflicted upon him as a thorn in the flesh."[17] Paul had labored extra for them. He made two visits to their city, spent well over two years there and was looking to visit a third time (2 Corinthians 12:14). Paul goes to great lengths for them. He even extends himself to the point of making a fool of himself (2 Corinthians 12:11). After all this, they are still shameful in behavior, sensual, argumentative and aloof (1 Corinthians 12). So McCant says that Paul's "thorn" is Corinth.

It seems that McCant is stretching the argument a bit. Paul is writing to the Corinthians this second time to encourage them, not to tell them what a headache they are. If the "thorn" was *rejected apostleship* or the *Corinthian Church* in general, then Paul's statement is an irrelevant insult to the Corinthians. Why would he write to encourage and instruct, then add "by the way, you people are a real pain" as a salutation? If this were the case, then Second Corinthians is irrelevant to all Christians who need encouragement. It would therefore be irrelevant in regard to divine healing. If this "thorn" were an exterior problem, why does Paul refer to it as "in the flesh"? This greatly weakens the possibility of Paul's thorn being "rejected apostleship" or the church at Corinth.

By Paul leaving his "thorn in the flesh" a mystery ("thorn" actually means "stake" or "spike"), it retains its universal application to anyone in difficulty. The "thorn in the flesh" broadens our understanding of how faith can work in our lives whether our difficulties are removed or not. Paul writes to encourage those in the church who are struggling with a problem or pain that God is not quickly alleviating. Paul's experience with the "thorn" tells of how God works victory in anything that is surrendered to Him.

While Satan is in the business of taking God's good things and making them bad, God is in the business of taking what Satan has wrecked and making it good again. So Satan in his usual way, full of intelligence yet bereft of insight, feverishly works ruin. In trials such as Paul's "thorn in the flesh," God can conquer by healing a situation or by working within the unfortunate circumstance to accomplish His purpose and for the sufferer's good.

A modern-day example is Joni Eareckson Tada. She was active and healthy before an accident that broke her neck and left her a quadriplegic. As it has turned out, she has a ministry that has blessed hundreds of thousands of people. Her ministry might not have been as effective had she not been confined to a wheelchair. She may not have had a ministry at all. But she was "slain" and yet she held onto her hope (see Job 13:15).

The simple lesson is that God can overrule in anyone's unfortunate situation to create a great testimony to His glory. That is, God can glorify Himself through what humans consider unfortunate. He does not need ideal conditions to accomplish His will.

It is not accurate to say that all health is God's direct doing and all sickness is Satan's direct doing. Surely Satan wanted to keep men like Stalin, Mao and Idi Amin healthy. They produce more evil when they are strong. Sociologists and criminologists have found two common traits among those who are socially deviant: robust health and good vision. The question is: Would a criminal have the capability to commit as many crimes if he, for example, had a congenital hip and very poor sight? Probably not.

The quandary is that some people are more godly when they are infirm and some are more ungodly when they are healthy. God wants godliness first. Yes, healing frees a person to praise and serve God more. Consequently, for those who are inclined to do evil, a healing would free them up to create more havoc. Some remain thankless and self-possessed even though God heals them. We see this clearly among the 10 lepers who received healing from Christ. Nine failed to return gratitude (Luke 17:11-19).

All of these factors must be taken into account in the ministry of healing. And by examining the "thorn in the flesh" concept we become aware that things are not as simple as we might suppose. As Paul's suffering served to further God's work through him, Christians today need not feel they are being punished when suffering. God can and will bring glory out of it.

4. The Effect of the Asclepian Healing Temples in Paul's Day

Some scholars speculate that Paul did not stress divine healing for the body because the Greek and Roman world in which he ministered was obsessed with the body and health. The Greco-Roman world had Asclepius, the legendary god of physicians. Asclepian temples were found throughout the empire. These temples were a solace for the pagan world. "Asclepius was presented as the most human-loving of the gods."[18] But unlike Christ, Asclepius healed only virtuous people.

The Asclepian sanctuaries had three essential components: a temple for sacrifice, a well or spring for washing and purification and a place for sleeping. The directors did their best to create a healing atmosphere. Everett Ferguson writes, "The sacred precincts included trees, baths, a theatre, a gymnasium, and sometimes a library, similar to a modern health or resort spa."[19] Sometimes extensive rest or exercise would be prescribed for healing. The Asclepian temples used everything they could to invoke physical healing.

Several reports mentioned the licking of the diseased spot by a snake or a dog. Other cures can be accounted for on psychological grounds or from the medical practice of the time. In the early period the priests employed surgery, drugs, and hypnosis; later, they effected cures by courses of treatment, including beneficent prescriptions like diet, exercise, baths, and medicines. In some cases the treatment prescribed was contrary to all ancient medical theory. . . . Magic was also employed for healing purposes.[20]

These methods of healing had nothing to attract the Greeks or Romans who had recently believed on Christ. They had lived their lifetime in the bondage of those pagan practices and rejoiced to be free of them. Nothing in the New Testament indicates that the Asclepian temples or any other form of animistic healing (and there were others) affected Paul's ministry of healing. He did not work from a theoretical base either in his ministry or in his writing. Paul was an experienced practitioner. He had had a widespread healing ministry in many cities of the Roman empire. There is a distinction between his healing ministry as a missionary and his writings which were devoted to the instruction of the Church. The Corinthian Church, founded by Paul, excelled in gifts, and obviously the gifts of healings were manifested in that congregation.

The scriptural data does not support the theory that Paul was restrained in writing about healing because of his concern for the influence of the Asclepian temples on the Christians. The Book of Acts details marvelous public healings in Paul's church-planting ministry. Consequently, the churches he founded practiced healing from their beginning. There was only a limited need for instruction on the doctrine of healing to such churches.

James' Teaching on Healing

James wrote from a pastoral perspective on the practice of divine healing. Anointing with oil was the usual way to administer healing in the assembly. This procedure did not negate the exercise of the gifts of healing. With James' instructions congregations knew that God's touch for the body was readily available. James' epistle, with the Gospels and the writings of Paul on healing, makes a complete doctrine of the practice of divine healing.

Instituting the Exercise of Divine Healing

The Apostle James wrote:

> Is any one of you sick? He should call the elders of the church to pray over him and anoint him with oil in the name of the Lord. And the prayer offered in faith will make the sick person well; the Lord will raise him up. If he has sinned, he will be forgiven. Therefore confess your sins to each other and pray for each other so that you may be healed. The prayer of a righteous man is powerful and effective. (James 5:14-16)

James, under the inspiration of the Holy Spirit, put in writing what had been practiced from the days of Jesus. Mark 6:13 says, "They drove out many demons and anointed many sick people with oil and healed them." This passage indicates that the apostles received the practice of anointing from Christ their teacher. They were to do this for the sick.

A.B. Simpson asserts that James 5:14ff. means, "that *this is a command*. It ceases to be a mere privilege. It is a divine prescription for disease; and no Christian can safely dispense with it."[21] Being impressed with this doctrine, Simpson gathered about him a group of likeminded people committed to the ministry of healing. This group, the newly formed Christian and Missionary Alliance, boldly practiced prayer for the sick according to James 5. Taking this James 5 passage as for today's Church, they preached Christ as the Great Physician.

There are three aspects of healing that are pivotal in James' orders. They are the elders, the prayer and the oil. A confident understanding of these three elements was basic if divine healing was to be administered effectively in the Church.

a. The Role of the Elders

As James wrote it, if anyone was sick he should call the elders. A famous healer from Asia Minor or Jerusalem need not be summoned. These elders were to be the godly officials of the local church. They were to be men of bold faith and sensitive to the Spirit. "The term 'elder' should not be construed simply to mean a person of senior age . . . Though some elders would likely be of mature age, the main qualification was spiritual competence."[22]

Since the Holy Spirit distributes the gifts according to His will and according to the ministry assigned in the Body, elders would certainly have gifts of healing. Healing, from anything we learn in the New Testament Scriptures, could not be ministered by mere position or office. Christ alone is Healer and the elders are only His chosen representatives empowered by His Spirit and gifts.

b. *The Role of Prayer*

In the Bible, sickness is usually a call to prayer. It was a way God got people's attention. An illness often meant take a "time-out" to talk with God or take a rest. (Today illness means take an aspirin!) And God, who desires fellowship and is constantly calling His own, sometimes needs to use an unpleasant circumstance. Therefore God wants His church to call out to Him when sickness strikes. The refusal to do so can be dangerous because it can lead to the progressive secularization of one's theological outlook. "The point James makes is that one ought not to complain or strike out, one ought not even to bear it with quiet resignation as the Stoics advised, but rather one should pray."[23]

When the elders anoint and pray, James says that "the prayer . . . will make the sick person well" (v.15). This is not a secret knowledge that only a few can understand. It is the releasing of the power of God. This "prayer offered in faith" opens up the situation to divine intervention. God will often not act before the prayer is offered up. Once healing has come, the patient and those ministering healing can be sure that the healing has come from God. Healing is then cause for thanksgiving and praise. The final results are enhanced relationships, vertical and horizontal.

James, in writing this instruction, is aware that co-laboring with God changes a person. God could have continued the ministry of healing by the divine touch of a select few. But by involving the elders, the elders then search their own hearts (instead of searching for some healer-man), desiring personal purity and righteousness and thus becoming fervent in their pursuit of God.

James is exhorting the flock to offer prayers of faith to God from righteous hearts. And God will even use sickness to accomplish this. The result is that the Church will grow to love and know God more.

c. *The Meaning of the Oil*

Exactly what is the meaning of the oil? Is it a medicine? Is it a cultic ritual? Is the anointing symbolic? Is it necessary?

Ralph Martin said that oil could have been included for a practical purpose such as medicine. He says, "Rituals with oil for healing were common in the ancient world."[24] Jesus tells of using oil for healing in the story of the good Samaritan.

James, under the inspiration of the Holy Spirit, put into writing what had been practiced from the days of Jesus. Mark 6:13 speaks of the 12 disciples' activity after they had been sent out to preach and deliver people from evil spirits. It says, "They drove out many demons and anointed many sick people with oil and healed them." This Mark passage indicates that the apostles received the practice of anointing from Christ their teacher.

This historical introduction of anointing with oil for healing in Mark 6:13 also helps our understanding of the purpose for anointing. The verb "anoint" is in the aorist tense, indicating an instantaneous act. This argues against the interpretation that the oil was intended as a medication. Medicine heals gradually and not instantaneously.

The anointing oil is representative of Christ the Anointed One. The application of the oil in His name brings all honor to Christ as Healer. Martin also surmises that the oil may have been applied by the elders to help in stimulating faith. The oil is not a guarantee of recovery but a sign of submission to God so He may work. The "finished product" and God's timing in finishing His work is His option.

The anointing of oil was by no means cultic. For the word "anoint" James uses a derivative of *aleiphein*. *Chriein* is another word for "anoint" in the New Testament, but Martin says that *chriein* is always used in a metaphorical sense.[25] "*Aleiphein* thus may have been chosen . . . because of standard usage yet still with the intention of conveying the thought that the anointing of oil was symbolic."[26] This would mean that there is nothing mysterious or cultic in James' orders to use oil.

The oil would only mean that the Lord is now here to heal and that it is time to exercise faith. James' use of *aleiphein* also discourages the possibility of the oil being a medicine.

James includes the section about sins being forgiven as confession is made, urging congregants to confess to each other and pray for each other so that forgiveness and healing can take place. Confession and repentance are crucial for someone seeking healing. The Holy Spirit will not bless over unconfessed sins. This is consistent with the rest of Scripture.

Verse 15 of the James passage assures, "And the prayer offered in faith will make the sick person well; the Lord will raise him up. If he has sinned, he will be forgiven." "The Lord will raise him up" is a promise that God will act.

So what is the church to make of those who are prayed for and yet remain sick? Many scholars have pondered this issue. James said *He* (God) will raise them up. Is healing always immediate? At least one answer to this dilemma is the fact that James 5:15 is a conditional promise. There is a possibility that the individual anointed with oil and prayed over by the elders may not have repented of a known sin, or may have had an unresolved controversy with a brother in the assembly or was insufficiently instructed to place vital faith in God's promise. Any of these conditions would account for the failure to receive healing. It is not beyond the realm of possibility that God for a sovereign reason delayed the healing. Healings are not always immediate. Some very spectacular healings have been gradual. James confidently states, "The Lord will raise him up." Note that *when* the Lord raises the sick is not the issue to James.

The pastor and elders must not abandon these orders because they are not sure when the Lord is going to act. God's promise of action is to trigger the response of prayer. If the Lord commands prayer then the church must exercise the requisite of praying and anointing in the name of the Lord. Neglect or omission out of fear of failure is disobedience.

James teaches that the healing ministry of Jesus Christ is to be carried on by the Church of Jesus Christ. And until further notice there is to be no wavering, doubting, excusing or ceasing from this activity.

Endnotes

1. Francis MacNutt, *Healing* (Notre Dame, IN: Ave Maria Press, 1974), 80.

2. For the disciples, "doing likewise" did not necessarily mean to duplicate Jesus' ministry. One Jesus was sufficient. However, what this did mean was that they were to be Spirit-directed and Spirit-empowered in their ministry as Jesus was.

3. Marion L. Soards, *The Apostle Paul: An Introduction to His Writings and Teaching* (New York: Paulist, 1987), 90.

4. Ibid., 38.

5. Ibid.

6. Ibid., 39.

7. Ibid.

8. Ibid., 40.

9. Ibid., 278.

10. Soards, 184-185.

11. Victor Paul Furnish, *Second Corinthians*, Anchor Bible Series, Vol. 32A (Garden City, NY: Doubleday, 1984), 548.

12. Ibid., 548.

13. Ralph P. Martin, *Second Corinthians*, Word Bible Commentary, vol. 40 (Waco, TX: Word, 1986), 414.

14. Ibid., 415.

15. Furnish, 549.

16. Jerry W. McCant, "Paul's Thorn of Rejected Apostleship," *New Testament Studies* 34:551.

17. Ibid., 572.

18. Everett Ferguson, *Backgrounds of Early Christianity*, (Grand Rapids, MI: Eerdmans, 1987), 174.

19. Ibid., 175-176.

20. Ibid., 177.

21. A.B. Simpson, *The Gospel of Healing* (New York: Christian Alliance Publishing, 1888; re-

print, Camp Hill, PA: Christian Publications, Inc., 1984), 25 (page reference is to reprint edition).

22. Ralph P. Martin, *James,* Word Biblical Commentary, vol. 48 (Waco, TX: Word, 1988), 207.

23. Peter H. Davids, *The Epistle of James* (Grand Rapids, MI: Eerdmans, 1982), 192.

24. Martin, 208.

25. Ibid., 208-209.

26. Ibid.

Chapter 4

Healing in Modern Times

The formation of The Christian and Missionary Alliance at the close of the 19th century brought a fresh demonstration of the Church's doctrine of healing for the body. The founder of the Alliance, A.B. Simpson, by his own personal testimony and his widely read books, attracted many people to the doctrine of divine healing.

The truth of "Christ Our Healer" was made known to Simpson many years after he experienced Christ as his Savior. Simpson ministered for years as a very weak and frail man before learning to trust Christ as Healer of his physical body.

He had learned of the renewal of healing going on in Europe, Great Britain and the United States at that time but was cautious about accepting it. It was a pilgrimage of many difficult years that finally brought A.B. Simpson to accept Jesus Christ as his Healer.

A. *The Pilgrimage of A.B. Simpson*

Simpson's healing pilgrimage began with his

constant battle with sicknesses. He had once witnessed the healing of a paralyzed man in his beginning days as a pastor. This sparked interest in
Simpson for personal healing. One leading parish-
ioner in his congregation, however, quickly
squelched his faith by encouraging him to doubt
the authenticity of the healing. It was not until
years later when he opened himself to personal
healing that his convictions became firm.

1. Constant Illness

As a young man, Simpson learned that "much
study wearies the body." His first physical breakdown occurred when he was a student in high
school. Determined to do well, he worked himself
to exhaustion. Simpson says of these days:

> Beginning a life of hard intellectual labor at
> the age of fourteen, I broke hopelessly down
> with nervous exhaustion while preparing for
> college. For many months I was not
> permitted by my doctor even to look at a
> book. During this time I came very near
> death. On the verge of eternity I gave myself
> at last to God.[1]

It is interesting that it was sickness and a near-
deathbed setting that drove him to salvation in
Christ. It was a prophetic experience. Little did he
know that nearly 25 years later he would begin to
minister Christ's healing to others who were sick,
hurting and dying in New York City.

At 21 years of age he was a college graduate and
pastor of a large church in Hamilton, Ontario. His

ambition to study and minister effectively nearly killed him again. Of his first pastorate Simpson writes, "Plunging headlong into my work, I again broke down with heart trouble and had to go away for months of rest, returning at length, as it seemed to me at the time, to die."[2]

He partly recovered from this second collapse. But the now feeble Simpson became a candidate for endless medicine.

> I labored on for years with the aid of constant remedies and preventives. I carried a bottle of ammonia in my pocket and would have taken a nervous spasm if I had ventured out without it.[3]

Because of his dependence on medicine, he even preached a sermon entitled, "My Medicine Chest."[4] He was always weak. Even a simple flight of stairs posed a threat. After such a feat, he says, "an awful and suffocating agony would come over me, and the thought of that bottle as a last resort quieted me."[5] Once, while in Switzerland, he climbed a flight of steps and thought he was going to suffocate. He vowed never to do such a thing again. He was a man chained to a faulty respiratory system. Gathering strength for ministry was a continual battle. In his own words:

> God knows how many hundreds of times in my earlier ministry, when preaching in my pulpit or ministering by a grave, it seemed

that I must fall in the midst of the service or drop into that open grave.[6]

Simpson's constant exhaustion was further punctuated by two other total collapses in health. Like the one in his teens, and at 21 during his first pastorate, these were also long-term breakdowns. It seemed "that the last drops of life were ebbing out."[7] Simpson had a burning heart for God and lofty visions, but his health was taking him down a dead-end street.

He was frustrated with the weakness that hampered his ministry. He did not like being thought of as "frail." To him it was depressing. His congregation knew of his problem. "My good people always thought me 'delicate.' I grew weary of being sympathized with every time they met me. The parishioners excused many a neglected visit because I was 'not strong.' "[8]

Simpson moved from Canada to a pastorate in Louisville, Kentucky. He continued to suffer debilitating health. He had yet to learn the truth of Christ as his Healer.

2. *Positive and Negative Influences for Healing*

Simpson witnessed a divine healing while pastoring in Louisville. Thompson writes, "He had been deeply impressed by the healing of a young paralytic in his congregation."[9] At the time Simpson witnessed this healing, he himself was struggling with poor health. He thought, "If God could heal this man's paralysis, then he could perhaps heal me!" Simpson says of this incident:

> The impression produced by this incident never left my heart. Soon afterwards I attempted to take the Lord as my Healer, and for a while, as long as I trusted Him, He sustained me wonderfully.[10]

His health would have been preserved and the years of illness would never have been, except for two factors. Simpson confessed,

> Being entirely without instruction, and advised by a devout Christian physician that it was presumption, I abandoned my position of simple dependence upon God alone, and so floundered and stumbled for years.[11]

Simpson had gained a mustard-seed faith, but no sooner had he gained this faith than it was nullified by bad advice.

3. The Inspiration to Receive Healing

In the mid-summer of 1881, while the Simpson family was vacationing in Old Orchard, Maine, Dr. Charles Cullis, a Christian physician from Boston, was conducting healing services there. He was instrumental in turning Simpson's doubt into faith again. In his practice, Dr. Cullis would pray for patients as well as employ his medical knowledge to assist in the healing process. "Some terminally ill patients had remarkable recoveries."[12] For this reason Dr. Cullis studied divine healing further, and became convinced that God wanted to heal the whole man.

One evening Simpson attended a service that Dr. Cullis was conducting where he "listened to at least 200 people give accounts of their healing. [Simpson recalls] 'I had believed that there were cases of healing—but the facts did not convince me.' "[13] Simpson considered himself very committed to Scripture and not one to be swayed by people's experiences. But that same night, his doubts about divine healing began to melt. For it were these testimonies that sent him to the Scriptures to examine the matter anew.

Simpson resolved that if he found healing for his body in the Scriptures he would accept it as true. "I determined that I must settle this matter one way or the other."[14] He wanted an answer about divine healing and received it that day. "At His feet, alone . . . I became convinced that this was part of Christ's glorious Gospel for a sinful and suffering world."[15] Roughly 15 years after he trusted his soul to the resurrected Christ, he now trusted his body to the resurrected Christ.

B. The Healing of A.B. Simpson

Simpson's healing was a life-changing experience for him. Divine healing played an important role in his personal life and preaching ministry.

Chapter 4

1. His Covenant of Healing

For A.B. Simpson healing was not an empty theory. He accepted Christ as Healer and made a definite covenant with God to trust Him for healing:

> And so one Friday afternoon at the hour of three o'clock, I went out into the silent pine woods—I remember the spot—and there I raised my right hand to heaven and made to God . . . these three great and eternal pledges:

1. I solemnly accept this truth as part of Thy Word and of the Gospel of Christ, and . . . I shall never question it until I meet Thee there.

2. I take the Lord Jesus as my physical life, for all the needs of my body until all my life-work is done. . . .
   I shall never doubt that He does become my life and strength from this moment and will keep me under all circumstances until all His will for me is perfectly fulfilled.

3. I solemnly promise to use this blessing for the glory of God and the good of others, and to so speak of it or minister in connection with it in any way in which God may call me or others may need me in the future.[16]

He arose from his covenant of prayer a renewed man of God. "Every fibre of my soul was tingling with a sense of God's presence. . . . It was so glorious to believe it simply, and to know that . . . He had it in hand."[17] He had now accepted Christ as his Healer and was soon to learn the testing his new covenant would bring.

2. The Testings That Came

Simpson's first test was doubting, the same test he had yielded to 15 years before. Wavering immediately as to the certainty of his commitment to Christ as his Healer, he was quickly reminded that this matter was settled forever. God had led him to this point. Simpson says, "I saw that when a thing was settled with God, it was never to be unsettled. . . . It was never to be undone or done over again."[18]

The second test came two days later. That Sunday he was asked to preach at a congregational church in New Hampshire. The Holy Spirit wanted him to testify what He had done in his life that same weekend. But Simpson was afraid to publicly take this stand. He confesses, "I tried to preach a good sermon of my own choosing."[19] He intended to deliver a normal, respectable sermon. The results were abysmal. "My jaws seemed like lumps of lead, and my lips would scarcely move."[20] He concluded the service as briskly as possible, went into a field and asked God to forgive him. He was given another chance that evening. Back in his hotel he spoke at a small service. He told them, "I had lately seen the Lord Jesus in a deeper fullness, as the Healer of the body, and had taken Him for myself."[21] He stammered, but was obedient.

112

The third test came on Monday. He was invited to climb Mt. Kearsarge in New Hampshire. It was 3,000 feet high! Instantly his mind flashed back to when he was left gasping for air in Switzerland. For decades a simple flight of stairs had winded him terribly. He had the enormous fear of verifying his healing and "shrank back at once."[22] Then he realized that not going would be to doubt God's healing. "I told God that in His strength I would go."[23]

He commenced hiking and the weakness came over him as always. But against this he grew distinctly aware of the presence of God. "When I reached the mountaintop, I seemed to be at the gate of heaven, and the world of weakness and fear was lying at my feet."[24] He had taken Jesus Christ as his strength. Now, for the first time in many years, he really knew what that meant.

Then came the fourth and most difficult test. Not long after coming home from New England, his three-year-old daughter Margaret was stricken with diphtheria. Mrs. Simpson wanted to call a doctor. The Simpsons had lost their son, Melville, to diphtheria at the same age. It was the repeat of a nightmare. Against his wife's insistence, Simpson did not call a doctor.[25] According to medical knowledge, Margaret would not last another day. He recalls, "With trembling hand I anointed her brow and claimed the power of Jesus' name."[26] Simpson remained at Margaret's bedside praying through the night. She was well by morning.

By now Simpson realized that God was breaking through a barrier in his mind. He had personally experienced the reality of God's healing. He was now able to minister the message of healing to others.

C. The Results of Healing

Simpson's covenant of healing transformed his life. His newfound strength for ministry launched him to a whole new level. Healing meetings occurred weekly. A healing home was opened. Along with these positive changes came ridicule and rejection from others.

1. New Strength for Ministry

Strength for ministry was very important to Simpson. The weakness he experienced prior to being healed was his main frustration in ministry. He was aware of and grateful for his new anointing to do God's work. He wrote, "I am intensely conscious, with every breath, that I am drawing my vitality from a directly supernatural source and that it keeps pace with the calls and necessities of my work."[27]

Simpson remembered the exhaustion he experienced in early years and likened his new strength to pouring oil on the dying embers of a fire. With his usual verbal flair, Simpson describes the joy of renewed health:

As God poured His fullness on my exhausted frame, a divine strength came, full

of sweet exhilaration and unwearied buoy-
ancy and energy, and in that light and life of
God I am working without exhaustion, and
trust still to work in His glorious all suffi-
ciency until my work is done.[28]

Simpson used his vigor to the full extent in the
Lord's work. The 38 years following God's touch
upon his body were a marvel. The amount of
work that Simpson accomplished in these years
was staggering. Tozer felt that the volume of work
Simpson amassed in life may well have only been
surpassed by John Wesley and the apostle Paul.[29]

2. The Friday Healing Meetings

After he was healed, Simpson committed himself to the ministry of divine healing. Now back in
New York, he commenced upon a healing ministry that would last nearly four decades and end up
playing a significant role in America's church history. The news about his physical healing and that
of his daughter Margaret's spread quickly. Soon
other people came to be healed. The number of
those interested became so large that a regular
meeting would need to be established.

Simpson was excited and challenged by this. At
the same time, he was concerned that it should not
dominate the Sunday services. Simpson also felt
that many weekly churchgoers were not prepared
for such events. Therefore he chose Friday as the
day for his healing meetings. This kept them ac-
cessible, yet slightly obscure. The meeting proved

to be a powerful tool for reaching people. Soon "the Friday afternoon meeting became a shrine for thousands of people connected with the churches of the city and its suburbs."[30] These meetings grew to be the largest weekday religious meetings in New York.[31]

Knowing that people were inclined to sensationalize healing and make a carnival of the supernatural, Simpson kept a tight check on these services. He was not concerned about the meetings becoming lackluster, but that Christ be the focus of these healing gatherings. He knew that God would be glorified through these healing services, so he deliberately chose Friday—a notoriously unpopular time for Christians to gather. "Though Simpson was cautious as to the time and place of healing meetings, miraculous cures that electrified the audience . . . occurred in [these] large public gatherings."[32]

His only concern was that a proper perspective be maintained by the participants. He knew what it was to think too little of divine healing—this was the story of the first 38 years of his life. Simpson did all he could to maintain a balance in his healing ministry. He had a concern for the people who needed teaching and counseling to receive healing for their physical conditions. This led to the realization of a plan to minister to them.

3. Berachah Healing Home

Simpson had learned of successful "healing homes" in Germany; Switzerland; London; Boston; and Buffalo, New York. His knowledge of these healing homes inspired him to begin one in New York City. Therefore, less than two years after Simpson's healing, the Berachah Home was opened for those needing more instruction and counsel. Many would require this before receiving healing.

The situation at Berachah was the inspiration for his first book, *The Gospel of Healing*. The book is a collection of eight articles written between 1883 and 1888. It was slightly revised in 1915. Interestingly enough, however, Simpson never changed his views on the subject. In the introduction, John Sawin tells of Simpson's grace, wisdom and tact in the ministry of healing.

> Simpson refused to impose his views of healing on others. He taught the truth as he saw it and experienced it. He only desired that his auditors or readers would understand the teaching, then examine the truth for themselves. If and when they were personally convinced and ready in heart and mind to commit themselves irrevocably to the Lord for His divine life, then and only then did Simpson consider them ready to be anointed and prayed for.[33]

Simpson had heavenly patience and a desire to wait on the Lord. He did not want even one person to enter into a covenant of healing with insufficient understanding. It was this concern that led to the writing and publishing of *The Gospel of Healing*.

Chapter 1 gives the scriptural foundation for healing. From Satan's work in the fall of man through the Old Testament to Christ and His commissioning, Simpson gives a brisk tour of the teaching on health that is threaded through the Word of God. Chapter 2 instructs in the principles of divine healing. In this chapter he includes his view of healing in the atonement. Chapter 3 covers the popular objections to healing, while chapter 4 gives practical direction to those seeking God's healing. Chapters 5 and 6 are selected testimonies from the Scriptures. In chapter 7 Simpson gives his own personal testimony. Chapter 8 is a testimony to the work of healing that had occurred recently and was now in progress.

If any came to this healing home with little knowledge of divine healing, they were requested to read *The Gospel of Healing* before prayer was offered on their behalf.

The opening of Berachah Home ("house of blessing") in May 1883 was financed by a gift of $2,000. One year later it was moved to a larger building in Manhattan. At this time, the home was put under the direction of two godly women: Ellen Griffin and Sarah Lindenberger. In March 1890, Berachah was moved again to a six-story building next to the New York Gospel Tabernacle on West 44th Street. In 1897 Miss Griffin died. That same year the Ross Taylor Home in Nyack was purchased and enlarged to become the new Berachah Home. Miss Lindenberger ran the home and ministered healing to still hundreds and hundreds more until her death in 1921.[34]

4. Ridicule and Rejection from Others

For Simpson, the joy of ministering healing was not without rejection from peers and others who were less open to such ministry. The Friday meetings were very successful, and the Berachah Home was a lighthouse of love for the hurting. But "by many others, he was vilified and ridiculed as another quack miracle worker."[35] His zeal for the Lord no doubt left him open to criticism from the hyper-conservative and the jealous alike. Yet in obedience to the Lord, Simpson continued his healing ministry, and the criticism of some only worsened.

Ironically, his critics were willing to let him alone as long as he struggled along sickly and weak. But when he became healthy, strong and energetic, they bitterly criticized his ministry and motives.[36]

By his own testimony "the penalty most costly to him for his healing was a sense of loneliness."[37] It reminded him of the loneliness he felt after being filled with the Holy Spirit. Back then his friends did not understand. They were not so intensely interested in spiritual matters. And now, in his pilgrimage with Jesus, Simpson again had to proceed alone. In short, Simpson felt deserted. As before, "the same sense of isolation overtook Simpson in the matter of healing."[38] He sums up his feeling of desertion:

> My old friends seemed to leave me and for months I seemed to be alone—separated from hundreds and thousands of ministers and people I had loved and worked with all my life. I felt I did not know them now and they did not know me as before.[39]

Even in all the human loneliness, his faith in Jesus never wavered. Jesus met him and ministered sustenance to him without fail.

The View of Healing That Developed

Through the changes in his life and the ridicule that Simpson experienced, a clear view of healing developed. In his view, healing was not for personal advancement but for living the life and continuing the work of the Lord Jesus Christ.

Simpson spells out his idea of "Christ Our Healer" in chapter 3 of *The Fourfold Gospel*, which is the compendium of Christian and Missionary Alliance distinctives. It was also Simpson's third book teaching divine healing. In chapter 3, Simpson begins by dispersing myths about healing and gives the 10 things that divine healing is not:

1. Divine healing is not medical healing. Simpson had no trouble with people using medicine. He

suggested they remain on medication unless directed otherwise by the Lord.

2. Divine healing is not metaphysical healing. It is not mind cure or Christian Science.

3. Divine healing is not magnetic healing in which a mysterious current flows from one body to another.

4. Divine healing is not spiritualism. Calling on any spirit other than Jesus Christ is *not* divine healing.

5. Divine healing is not prayer cure. This idea has the vague idea that if enough humans band together and pray, God, as if to be swayed by democracy, will finally get the message, bend His stubborn will and heal that person.

6. Divine healing is not faith cure. God does the healing, not the faith. (Faith is the avenue to healing that must be placed in Christ the Healer.)

7. Divine healing is not cure by will power. Divine healing is a work from the divine, not the victim.

8. Divine healing is not defiance of God's will, as if to say, "I will have this . . . whether He wills it or not!"

9. Divine healing is not physical immortality. It is fullness of life until the life work is done.

10. Divine healing is not mercenary healing. One could not adopt divine healing as a professional trade just like any other job; God's gifts are free.

The above 10 points helped clear the atmosphere of what some might read into his doctrine on healing.

He continues with what divine healing is:

1. Divine healing is the supernatural divine power of God infused into human bodies, renewing their strength and replacing the weakness of suffering human frames by the life and power of God.

2. Divine healing is founded on the Word of God alone. Human reason, intellect, testimony and dedication are less than worthless, if not founded on the Word of God.

3. Divine healing is always done in submission to and within the will of God. Simpson warned people against fighting that will, if indeed their life work was complete.

4. Divine healing is part of the redemptive work of Jesus Christ. It is partly the reason for the incarnation; the foundation of healing being in the cross.

5. Divine healing comes through the life of the resurrected Christ, who bodily rose from the dead.

6. Divine healing is the healing that comes via the work of the Holy Spirit. Jesus healed by the

Holy Spirit while on earth, and He is still the same today.

7. Divine healing is based on God's grace, not man's work or merit. It is a free gift that must be received.

8. Divine healing comes by faith. God does the healing, yet it is faith that enables healing to take place.

9. Divine healing is in accordance with all the facts of church history. There are endless examples of God's continuous healing hand at work from Paul to the present.

10. Divine healing is one of the signs of the age. It is the forerunner of Christ's coming and proof of God's power.

Servanthood and submission to Jesus Christ are primary in Simpson's view on divine healing. The blessings received are life-changing, for His glory and for the purpose of building up the church.

1. Healing as Obedience and Not for Self-Gain

Simpson was not a crowd-pleaser. He refused to deliberately attach "the sensational" to the ministry of divine healing. He was careful never to use his gift to fill auditoriums or offering plates. From what he perceived:

It is very solemn ground and can never be made a professional business or a public parade. Its mightiest victories will always be silent and out of sight, and its power will keep pace with our humility and holiness.[40]

Had he emphasized it more, extremist groups would have been pleased. Had he emphasized it less, conservative groups would have been pleased. But he was concerned with godliness and obedience, not prestige or thrill shows. Thompson wrote of Simpson, "Had he renounced divine healing he could have obtained a wider and more tolerant recognition. But that would have required a diplomacy of which he could never be guilty."[41] Simpson had committed himself to following the Lord. And that is exactly what he did the remainder of his days.

2. *The Atonement and Resurrected Christ for the Body*

"Simpson taught that the basis of faith in divine healing was the atonement of Jesus Christ."[42] He took Isaiah 53 to mean healing as covering both soul and body. Divine life came from the resurrected Christ. This life was infused into our frame, should we accept it. Jesus was more than a spiritual blessing. Simpson stated, "Not only is His spirit for my spirit, but His body for my body, touching mine into life."[43] He called Jesus "my complete Savior for body as well as for soul."[44] Simpson did not have a "superman" or "fountain of youth" belief. Neither did divine healing grant one to perfect, trouble-free living.

The idea is too common that a person who is healed is thereafter immune from every kind of sickness. Dr. Simpson's conception of divine life for the body was exactly contrary to this supposition. He felt himself to be wholly dependent upon a vital and continuous connection with the Lord for his life.[45]

This blessing was God's doing and for His glory. For Simpson, divine healing is not "God at our disposal." It is our believing God and in faith putting ourselves at His disposal.

His book *The Lord for the Body*, published in 1903, rounded out his conviction on divine healing. It was a presentation of divine healing as found in different books of the Bible and characters in the Bible. It is not intended to be exhaustive, only a helpful guide. Subsequent printings added material, bringing the book to 15 chapters: chapter 12, "Natural and Supernatural Healing"; chapter 14, "Paul and Divine Healing" and chapter 15, "Inquiries and Answers (Concerning Divine Healing)."

Simpson is credited with enlightening countless people to the truth of divine healing. The notable change in the awareness and exercise of this truth during his era testifies to the effect of the one man, Simpson.

3. The Way to Receive Healing

Simpson taught that healing was available upon two conditions. First, the heart must be right with God. Second, the person must have faith. "If there is any sin . . . lay it at the Lord's feet, choose His

will in the matter."[46] "The holy Gospel only re-
mains in a holy life and heart."[47] After receiving
the Lord's forgiveness, one must still pursue healing in faith. Simpson saw the faith necessary for
healing in Jesus' day as no different from what is
necessary now. As retold in *Birth of a Vision*, "The
seeker must come to a definite point and cross it,
put down a stake and take it forever. He will say,
'this is God's truth and I stand upon it.' "[48]

4. Continued Signs and Wonders

In Simpson's teaching and writing he regularly
spoke of a "latter rain."[49] This motif alludes to the
Joel 2 passage concerning when the Spirit would
be poured out. The days of the apostles were the
early portion of the "rain."

> If the "early rain" had come at Pentecost ac-
> companied by supernatural manifestations
> of the Spirit such as tongues, miracles and
> prophecy, Simpson reasoned that one could
> rightly expect these "wonderful manifesta-
> tions" to be part and parcel of the "latter
> rain."[50]

If Joel 2 spoke of the Pentecost blessing following Christ and the first advent, then First Corinthians 12 meant there would be a continued
manifestation of gifts until the second advent.
Simpson felt that from his own day until Christ
returned, this "rain" would only intensify. He
called the cessationist theory[51] (the view that the

126

gifts of the Spirit had ceased) "one of the lies the devil sugar-coated . . . in the form of a theological maxim."[52] Whatever would be the reason God would withdraw His Spirit from the church? Simpson saw no reason for people to think Christ had left His Church to flounder until He returned.

According to Simpson, signs and wonders were a necessity in the modern-day church. God worked healing to bless individual Christians and the Church as a whole. He also saw healing as a great tool for evangelism. "Every generation of Christians needed 'a living Christ' to perform miracles that authenticated the gospel in the face of unbelievers."[53] Simpson further said, "We are in the age of miracles, the age of Christ, the age which lies between two Advents . . . the age of Power, the age which, above all other ages of time, should be intensely alive."[54]

Simpson felt that if we live for Christ, then our faith and works today need not be less than that of the apostles. It may not have been his original intention, but a new man had emerged as a burning example and catalyst for a modern-day healing ministry in the pattern of Jesus' healing ministry. The pilgrimage and prayer life of this one man inspired untold thousands of people to seek Christ anew. The discipleship he fostered was the headwaters for millions of future conversions, countless Bible studies, churches planted, missionaries launched and divine healings. At the time, Simpson had no idea that his passion for Christ and humble attitude of reckless obedience would ignite a movement whose effects are still being felt today.

Endnotes

1. A.B. Simpson, *The Gospel of Healing* (Harrisburg, PA: Christian Publications, Inc., 1915; reprint, Camp Hill, PA: Christian Publications, Inc., 1984), 107 (page references are to the 1984 edition).

2. Ibid.

3. Ibid., 108.

4. Robert J. Niklaus, John S. Sawin and Samuel J. Stoesz, *All for Jesus* (Camp Hill, PA: Christian Publications, Inc., 1986), 39.

5. Simpson, 108

6. Ibid.

7. Ibid.

8. Ibid.

9. A.E. Thompson, *A.B. Simpson: His Life and Work* (Harrisburg, PA: Christian Publications, Inc., 1960), 72.

10. Ibid.

11. Ibid.

12. Niklaus, Sawin and Stoesz, 40.

13. Ibid.

14. Thompson, 75.

15. Ibid.

16. Ibid., 75-76.

17. Ibid., 76.

18. Ibid.

19. Ibid., 77.

20. Ibid.

21. Ibid.

22. Ibid., 78.

23. Ibid.

24. Ibid.

25. Simpson did not oppose medicinal assistance. He himself had used medicine. He never counseled anyone to haphazardly discard their medication. The intensity of his experience with Margaret confirmed to Simpson that only at Christ's leading should someone cease using medicine.

26. Niklaus, Sawin and Stoesz, 42.

27. Thompson, 80.

28. Niklaus, Sawin and Stoesz, 42; quoted in A.W. Tozer, *Wingspread* (Harrisburg, PA: Christian Publications, Inc., 1943), 81.

29. Ibid.

30. David F. Hartzfeld and Charles Nienkirchen, eds., *The Birth of a Vision* (Alberta, Canada: Buena Book Services, 1986), 14.

31. Niklaus, Sawin and Stoesz, 55.

32. Ibid. 42.

33. Ibid.

34. Ibid., 43.

35. Ibid., citing A.B. Simpson, "What God Is Doing in Our Age," *The Word, the Work and the World* (July/August, 1885), 209.

36. Thompson, 140.

37. Ibid., 139.

38. Hartzfeld and Nienkirchen, eds., 12.

39. Thompson, 63.

40. Ibid., 64.

41. Ibid., 79.

42. Hartzfeld and Nienkirchen, eds., 14; citing A.B. Simpson, *The Word, the Work and the World* (July/August, 1885), 205.

43. Ibid, 13; citing A.B. Simpson, *The Word, the Work and the World* (July/August, 1887), 75.

44. Ibid.; citing A.B. Simpson, *The Word, the Work and the World* (July/August, 1885), 204.

45. Ibid., 132; citing A.B. Simpson, "Editorial," *Living Truth* (December, 1906), 706; and "Spiritual Sanity," *Living Truth* (April, 1907), 191.

46. Ibid., 133; citing A.B. Simpson, *Earnests of the Coming Age* (New York: Christian Alliance Publishing Co., 1921), 118.

47. Ibid.

48. Ibid.; idem, *The Gospel of Healing*, 55, 57, (1915 edition, pages do not coincide with the 1986 edition).

49. Incidentally, his writings and preaching on the subject of the Holy Spirit and divine healing became the initial inspiration that started the Pentecostal movement. In fact, the founders of The Assembly of God denomination were a group of people directly instructed and inspired by A.B. Simpson. They were the ones who wanted even more emphasis on the gifts of the Spirit and all that it implied. And in 1906 they diverged from The Christian and Missionary Alliance to do so.

50. Hartzfeld and Nienkirchen, eds., 132; citing A.B. Simpson, "Editorial," *Living Truth* (December, 1906), 706; and "Spiritual Sanity," *Living Truth* (April, 1907), 191.

51. Cessationist theory is the belief that signs and wonders faded away after the apostles.

52. Hartzfeld and Nienkirchen, eds., 133; citing A.B. Simpson, *Earnests of the Coming Age* (New York: Christian Alliance Publishing Co., 1921), 118.

53. Ibid.

54. Ibid.; idem, *The Gospel of Healing*, 55, 57 (1915 edition pages do not coincide with the 1986 edition).

Chapter 5

Healing Today

Is divine healing a relic of the past? Some feel that way. Here is a sample of some dubious comments I heard while doing the interviews: "We talk about divine healing, we pray about divine healing, but I wonder if we believe it anymore." A missionary commented, "There's a big gap between our theory and our practice." A young pastor said with concern, "I don't think the Church today has the childlike faith that A.B. Simpson had." A pastor on the West Coast lamented, "God's people are running to doctors before the Lord. We are so dependent on medicine. We are forgetting to go to the Lord. Anymore, He is a last resort." One missionary seemed alarmed, "From what I see, there is very little healing taught or practiced in the U.S. and Canada. We dilute and deny the Scriptures when we don't. It's getting dangerous."

While there is some truth in these comments they may be somewhat exaggerated for lack of information about dynamic churches that enjoy a healing ministry. The comments represent a perspective from persons who are not seeing in their own church life a demonstration of this truth.

There is a wide spectrum of experiences and emotions among us regarding healing ministry that ranges from zealous obedience to feelings of failure, resignation and dismissal. But wherever we find ourselves in this range, all of us acknowledge in varying degrees that God is real and active today. This truth should either confirm our present practices or inspire us to change our ways to be more like Christ's ways of caring for the hurting. One man testified:

It was the 1960s. A man brought one of his relatives to the mission station to receive help for an illness. The sick man was anointed for healing and prayed over. The sick man was divinely healed in the presence of witnesses. The man who brought him was overjoyed at the power of God.

The next day the same man brought a friend who was blind. He asked the missionary to also anoint *him* for the healing of his sight. The missionary became intimidated and told the man that he better get help elsewhere.

He admitted that he had retreated from duty. He said that, decades later, his lack of faith and decision not to anoint and pray for him back then still bothers him now.

As described above, many of us have thresholds to our faith. This is not a comfort but should arouse us to pray, "Lord, increase my faith." The following are inspiring stories of people who have personally experienced a dynamic healing touch from Christ's hand in the present day. If you are not already convinced of this awesome truth, the following stories should help illustrate that though Christ our Healer has ascended from the earth, He has not left and He has not changed:

Bertha Garrison
Sebring, Florida

On March 10, 1994, I entered the operating room at 7:00 a.m. to have an aorta valve replaced in my heart. I had been examined by two cardiologists and was informed that without an operation I had only six months to live. They decided I had a 50-50 chance of surviving. My husband, my two sons and our minister, Rev. James W. O'Hara, held a prayer meeting in the hallway of the hospital, asking for divine intervention. At 11:00 a.m., the surgeon called my family together and said, "Your prayer has been answered, she came through OK." Needless to say, they immediately went to God in thankful prayer. After a few hours in recovery, I was moved to Intensive Care Unit, but developed a leakage. After three units of transfusion, they were still trying to correct the leakage. More prayer and dependence on our Maker. At 10:00 p.m., Dr. Scott called my husband to obtain permission to open my chest again. More intercessory prayer. At midnight, Dr. Scott called my family to proclaim success! From Thursday morning to Sunday morning I knew nothing of all this, but God was working. The lines of prayer were kept constantly open by my family and numerous Christian friends. All through the ordeal my favorite Bible verse was Psalm 37:5: "Commit your way to the LORD; trust in him and he will do this."

In September of 1989 I noticed that I was gaining weight—about five pounds per week. Also I was not feeling well. After going to the doctor three times in one week, the problem could not be located. I had gained 15 pounds by this time. My doctor referred me to a gynecologist who, upon examination, discovered I had a fast-growing tumor. I went to church and was anointed for healing by our Pastor Charles Hartney and the elders. That week the doctor put me in the hospital. I did not know until the anesthesiologist came to my room that I was to have surgery in the morning. I refused surgery, informing him that I had been prayed for and anointed. The next morning I was transferred to Lakeland Medical Center and put through a series of tests. The radiologist found no tumor! I feel God answered our prayers as I traveled from one hospital to the next. Years later I still have no signs of a tumor. I have gone through deep valleys with the Lord but He has always held my hand and walked through them with me.

Gordon and Jane Kelly
Ellensburg, Washington

When our daughter Erica was 21 months old, we experienced an event which confirmed in our minds the healing power of Christ. Erica had an upper respiratory tract infection and was running a very high fever—106 degrees. Her mother Jane was watching her closely. Without warning, Erica started to convulse. She stopped breathing, her eyes rolled back and she turned blue. Jane scooped her up as we headed off to the hospital. As we got to the car, Jane lifted Erica and pleaded, "Jesus, help her!" Erica immediately began to breathe. We went on to the hospital where Erica spent the night being observed. The next morning, with her fever and infection gone, she went up and down the halls visiting other patients and bringing joy to them as only a toddler can.

When Erica was three years old, we began to notice that when she really tried to focus on something, she either closed one eye or one of them would "cross." Our concern motivated us to seek medical attention. In conjunction with this effort, we sought the prayers of other believers and our elders at the church. The opthalmologist's prognosis was not encouraging. Her eyes would not straighten with glasses. He prescribed a muscle relaxant, which appeared to work. It was a dangerous medication as it would synergize with another anesthetic, one which should be administered in an emergency. Erica had to wear a medical ID bracelet noting this fact. After a couple of years, she began to build a tolerance to this medication. The opthalmologist suggested taking her off the medication for two weeks in order to refract her eyes. He wasn't sure what to do because glasses still wouldn't keep her eyes straight. Again we asked believers to pray for God's intervention. She was in kindergarten at the time. Those two weeks were difficult because her eyes would cross so badly when she tried to focus. After this two week period, the doctor examined her and declared that her eyes would remain straight with only the help of glasses. He repeated the examination three times because he could not believe the glasses were keeping them straight. Jane stated that Erica had been prayed for. The doctor retorted, "I don't know about that, but her eyes are straight." They have been since 1977!

Myrna Ballard
Eastanollee, Georgia

Tabita, a young Red Bobo girl we knew, lived in Burkina Faso, Africa. She was a Christian and was attending a Bible Camp in a small village. One evening upon returning from a meeting, she was bitten by a viper, one of the deadliest snakes of West Africa. We were called and immediately went to the hut where she was lying on a mat. There was no anti-snake venom due to the lack of refrigeration. No doctors lived in the village or the whole area. Medical facilities were also unavailable. But God was there.

Praying for wisdom, we started suction in an attempt to remove the injected poison. Amidst the prayers by campers and the pastor, she started to bleed from her mouth and open sores on her body. This meant the venom had traveled throughout her body; death was coming closer. We spent the night alternating between praying and resting. God heard and answered. After a while the bleeding stopped, and although Tabita felt weak for a day or two, she was soon up. She returned to her normal routine, praising God for His healing touch on her body.

Stephen Renicks
Northport, Alabama

When I was 16, I was hospitalized with a duodenal ulcer. With medical treatment it was cured. However, I continued to suffer from frequent stomach discomfort especially when I was under a lot of stress. After graduating from Nyack College, I attended Jaffray School of Missions, the forerunner of the Alliance Theological Seminary. While there my wife and I began the process of becoming missionaries with The Christian and Missionary Alliance. One of the requirements was a medical examination. The physician reported that if I had a recurrence of the ulcer, an overseas assignment would not be recommended. It was 1972. Shortly after, I began to have all the symptoms of another ulcer. For three weeks the symptoms persisted and I was unable to eat without stomach pains. I did not go to a doctor because I was afraid of the result. One evening we attended a concert at Nyack College where the vocalist sang, "He Touched Me." While he was singing, I cried out to the Lord saying, "Lord, if there was ever a time that I needed Your touch, it is now." In that moment He touched me and healed me. I went home, ate a normal meal without stomach pain and have never had another problem.

Stelda Taylor
Newark, Delaware

During a service at Summit Grove Camp in New Freedom, Pennsylvania, the Holy Spirit convicted me of my problem with anxiety. I don't think the subject was even mentioned in the message, but I was strongly convicted. I went to the altar to ask God's forgiveness and for victory over this sin. Two people whom I did not know came to pray with me. When I explained my need, I did not mention I had colitis simply because I did not think of it. All the time the Holy Spirit was convicting me of this sin, it did not enter my mind that my anxiety and the colitis were connected.

After I prayed and the two strangers prayed for me, we stood up. Something very amazing happened—I don't know how to explain it—I felt nothing physically, I just knew I had been healed of colitis. I don't know if either of the two people noticed any change of expression on my face or not, but I stood only a matter of seconds. They stood quietly looking at me and then I softly whispered, "I have been healed of colitis." It was so wonderfully amazing to me, I had been forgiven and healed. Praise His holy Name! As the days and weeks passed I proved I was healed by eating corn on the cob and coleslaw, two of the delicious foods served there at the Summit Grove dining room that I had not been able to eat since contracting colitis.

Perhaps you would be interested in knowing I have several health problems. One in particular I have had most of my life and have been anointed and prayed for many times but have not been healed. However, this does not affect in any way the truth of my healing of colitis.

Rachel E. Lohonen
Minneapolis, Minnesota

It was 1970, and God decided to heal the deteriorated discs in my spine. It started back in 1967 when I had symptoms of pain and weakness in my lower back. My health became so poor that I continuously felt as if I had just worked a 24-hour shift. Everything prescribed by my orthopedic surgeon—traction, a brace, exercise and bed rest—did not change a thing. One day as I was memorizing Psalm 6, verse 2 caught my attention: "Be merciful to me, LORD, for I am faint; O LORD, heal me, for my bones are in agony." Through that verse, God revealed that He intended to heal me. I had gotten to where I couldn't walk without assistance, and I had to lie on a couch at church rather than sit in a pew. That summer, as was our family custom, we attended Big Sandy Camp. After one of my children had helped me to chapel one morning for prayer meeting, the camp evangelist stopped by my couch. He said to me, "Do you know what I feel like saying to you? . . . 'Silver and gold have I none, but such as I have give I thee: In the name of Jesus Christ of Nazareth rise up and walk." (Acts 3:6, KJV) I looked up at him and said, "That sounds like a good idea." He assured me he was serious, so I just got up and was able to walk alone. I am still praising God today for His healing power but most of all for salvation.

Lynn Carpenter
La Habra, California

No one will ever be able to tell me that the day of miracles is past. The Lord has shown me several times that this is not so, but never as strong as these two events.

On June 26, 1972, my son Jason was born in the early morning hours. After I nursed him at 6:00 a.m. he was taken out for some normal newborn procedures. At 6:00 that evening (I hadn't seen him all day), a nurse came to me and said Jason wasn't feeling well and they would feed him in the nursery. By 8:30 p.m. his pediatrician came to me looking very worried. He informed me they wanted to run some tests and that I needed to sign consent papers. He tried to reassure me, but the look on his face was not convincing. At 10:30 p.m. the doctor returned looking even more concerned and asked me to have my husband come to the hospital. I asked why and was told they were having trouble doing a spinal tap on Jason and wanted to transfer him to another hospital that specialized in neonatal care. Later we learned they had tried over 20 times, unsuccessfully, to get a spinal tap. They didn't want to believe it, but they were sure it was spinal meningitis. I called my husband, who came immediately. Up to this time, Jason's father had not even been able to hold him.

When we were signing papers authorizing the transfer, the nurses brought Jason to us, concerned he would not survive the ambulance ride. They were giving us a chance to hold our baby one last time. He had terrible jaundice and looked pitifully weak.

The ambulance left. My husband went home. I felt so alone and scared. Calling my prayer partner helped me to see the situation clearly as she advised me on what I had to do. God had given this child to me and I was to give him back. I prayed to God that His will be done and promised to raise Jason to know the Lord if he were given back to me. But if the Lord wanted Jason back He could have him. This seems so trite, but it was the hardest prayer I have ever prayed.

By the time Jason had arrived at the other hospital, his color had improved. When they did the spinal tap, his spinal column was completely clear. He was released three days later. A week after examining him completely all the pediatrician could do was shake his head. He told us that because of the problems he had seen the week before, he had expected Jason to be severely handicapped. Now, seeing the amazing results, there was no other explanation than a miracle!

When God heals, He doesn't mess around. Not only did He heal Jason from being handicapped, He gave him extraordinary athletic abilities. He was able to dribble a basketball at two. Jason was so talented in basketball that at the age of five he had high school coaches coming to watch him play. In high school, he was all-league in volleyball, basketball, football and baseball. In his senior year he was league Most Valuable Player (MVP) in football and team MVP in football and basketball. He was recruited by over 30 schools for athletic scholarships. I do not list these accomplishments to brag about my son, but to boast for my Lord. When He does something He does a great job. As we promised, we taught Jason that his abilities aren't his own, they come from the Lord. He has taken many opportunities to share his testimony with friends and teammates.

The second incident involves my daughter Amy. When Amy was 18 months old and Jason was five, we lived in a home with a swimming pool. It was a hot summer day and the kids and I were out enjoying the pool. Jason had two friends over and they were swimming in the deep end. Amy and I had been in the shallow end and decided to get out. I took off Amy's life vest and started to run water into the pool to replenish the water splashed out by the boys. I had a timer on the table and told the boys they could swim for five more minutes. The phone rang and I ran into the house to answer it.

As I was speaking to the mother of one of the boys, I heard a horrible scream. It was Jason, and I instantly knew what had happened. The timer had gone off and he was getting out to re-set it when he saw Amy lying at the bottom of the pool! He hastily grabbed her and got her to the steps by the time I reached the pool. I had never taken a CPR course but had seen it done several times. I did know how to pray and cried out, "Jesus, help me," and started to breathe for her. She was blue and very spongy. As I breathed, Satan whispered in my mind, "She's dead. You're doing it wrong." But I kept praying. All of a sudden she started to cry and spit up water. In the meantime, Jason had run next door where the neighbor called 911.

Amy was drifting in and out of consciousness when the paramedics arrived. They took her in the squad car, not wanting to wait for an ambulance. She was stabilized at the hospital and within 60 minutes you would have never known what had happened. She wanted to get up and play. We didn't know how long she went without breathing and the doctors couldn't give me much hope as to how this would affect her in the future.

In high school, Amy took honors classes in math, English and history and earned a grade point average of 3.7. Amy is also a talented volley-ball player whose team came in fifth in the nation at the Junior Olympics.

The Lord, in both of these incidents, did not require fancy prayers—just sincerity. I am so glad and eternally grateful I serve a living God who still performs miracles!

Don Mathis
Lilburn, Georgia

At first I had headaches which were just like any other. But they didn't stay that way long. After having a headache 24 hours around the clock for two months, I went to the doctor. After much testing and examination, our doctor told me my problem was caused by hypertension or high blood pressure. I went through four different medications, with the headache persisting all the while, and still had what the doctor called "high normal pressure." Finally I reached the point of absolute agony. Further tests revealed that the walls to one of the primary arteries in my brain had weakened as a result of the high blood pressure and had expanded to the point of applying pressure to the nerves and tissue around it. Then there was concern about the possibility of a rupture which my doctor said would most likely result in death. Medications were started as the condition was inoperable.

A few weeks later my alarm went off, preparing me for another day in the office—but I couldn't get up. The lower part of my back felt like someone had pushed an ice pick right through my spine. After giving me an examination, my doctor explained how the muscles in the lower part of my back had literally pushed everything out of place as a result of the stress and tension.

Soon after this I came down with pneumonia, strep throat and EBV II (a virus that basically disables your immune system along with various other ill effects). I was going downhill rapidly and nothing the field of medicine had to offer was having any effect. With so many things going wrong, I was missing more days than I was working and had no choice but to take a medical leave of absence starting April 1.

I had hoped that staying at home in bed would help, but it didn't. After two months in bed, I was much worse. Late in the evening on Tuesday, May 31, I had been lying on our sofa in much discomfort. With much weakness and difficulty, I climbed the stairs to go to bed in hopes of finding some relief. But when I lay down I felt overwhelmed by it all and didn't know how much more I could take. But I soon found out . . .

Around 3:00 a.m. I began to have hard sharp pains around my heart and had difficulty breathing. Within minutes I felt as if I were suffocating, and I knew, I just simply knew, I was not going to live to see the sun the next morning. My life was slipping away. I picked up my Bible, laid it on my chest and placed my hands across it. With tears in my eyes I cried out to our heavenly Father and prayed in the name of our Savior Jesus Christ that He cleanse and heal me. I prayed, "Oh Lord, please cleanse me and heal me," over and over and over again. Although I was not well, I felt at peace and fell asleep. Around 7:30 a.m. Wednesday I woke up, still holding my Bible over my heart. When I opened my eyes, I felt a wonderful, warm, tingling sensation from the top of my head to the tip of my toes. When I sat up I felt energy flowing into my body. When I stood up my eyes filled with tears, but they were not tears of pain—they were tears of joy. I knew that the Holy Spirit had touched me and had cleansed me and healed me. The headache was gone; the hurting in my back was gone; the virus and illness were gone; and my heart felt strong and wasn't hurting.

As I was getting dressed, my wife came to me, as she has had every morning since I became ill, and asked how I was doing. When I looked into her eyes, my eyes filled with tears that flowed like a river. I wanted to tell her how our precious heavenly Father had touched me with His wonderful healing power, but I couldn't speak through all the tears and emotion. Without knowing how our Savior had touched me, my tears frightened her. She held me close and said, "Don't worry, honey, no matter what else happens, God will see us through; sometimes it helps to let go and cry."

It took me a few minutes to get myself together enough to tell her how He had touched me and healed me. I had seen how worrying about me had taken its toll on her, but I didn't know what to do about it. But when I told her, "Sweetheart, you don't have to worry anymore because He has healed me," I could see the weight of the world leave her shoulders as we held each other and cried tears of joy.

Not only has He healed me, He has taken me to a spiritual level that is far higher than I have ever been before. He has filled my life with a beautiful, sweet peace and joy that goes far beyond anything I could have imagined or know how to put into words. I can feel the Holy Spirit working in me every day and can feel Him pulling me closer to His side. I feel a love that I have never felt before and have truly learned how He will make me first in His life if I make Him first in mine. Now I understand what it is like to have a love relationship with Him, one that is real and personal. It is hard to describe this beautiful closeness. All that matters anymore is my love for Him, my wife and my children.

It was fun to see the look on the doctor's face when he examined me and said, "All I can say is that you are healed. You are well! When do you want to go back to work?"

Bill Hunt
Ellensburg, Washington

I became a Christian in May 1959 while serving in the United States Air Force. We attended a small Nazarene Church in Big Springs, Texas. We had just had our first child in January. Tim was our delight and we were thrilled to be parents. I was discharged from the Air Force on November 3 of that year—and Tim contracted polio on November 23. He was in the hospital for three weeks.

When he was discharged he was paralyzed from the waist down. This was devastating to us, and all we could do was hold on to the Lord.

On January 23, 1960, our first daughter, Mona, was born. The doctor told my wife and me that something was wrong, but he could not make a diagnosis. In the summer of 1960 we heard of a therapist in Boise, Idaho, who worked with polio victims so we decided to move to Boise so that Tim could get the best therapy possible. While we were preparing to move, Mona died in her sleep. We were devastated. The coroner accused us of smothering her with a pillow. Our doctor was out of town and did not return for a week. When he returned, he was able to clear our names with the coroner because an autopsy showed a spinal block had been the cause of both her medical problems since birth and her death.

Things went well in Idaho and on March 21, 1961, our second son, Bill Jr., was born. On June 8, 1962, our third son, Daniel, was born. Bill Jr. developed ear problems at three months and had earaches most of the time. After his first birthday, we had to take him to the doctor every day to have his ear drums lanced. At about 1:30 one morning, I was walking the floor holding him. He had a fever and was crying. I knelt down and said, "Lord, I just can't take it anymore." Billy instantly stopped crying. I was fearful that he had died. I checked him, he was sleeping peacefully and his fever was gone. The Lord had completely healed him and he never had another ear problem. Praise the Lord!

When Daniel was about two years old he was in the back yard playing and put a glass under a leak in our furnace fuel barrel. He drank four ounces of diesel fuel. In checking on the boys, my wife discovered something was wrong and immediately rushed him to the hospital. The doctors pumped his stomach but said it was too late; he probably would not live over two hours. Once again God stepped in. Not only did he live, but today he is 6'4" and has amazing God-given talent as an artist!

On December 23, 1965, our daughter Joanna was born. After a minor complication with strep throat, she was able to go home, healthy; there were no problems!

On February 2, 1966, my wife had taken Joanna to the doctor for a checkup, she was doing great. Driving to school to pick up Tim, my wife hit a hole in the road and ran into a parked car. As a result, Jean, Bill Jr., Daniel and Joanna were put in the hospital. Jean and Bill Jr. had brain concussions, and Daniel was bruised. Joanna had suffered a fractured skull all the way around her head. The soft spot was swollen to the size of a hen's egg. She was in very serious danger, and the doctors had to insert large needles into the soft spot five times in a 24 hour period to relieve the pressure on the brain.

On the evening of February 3 my boys and I got down on our knees in the living room and asked God to heal her. A short time later I went to the hospital. The neurosurgeon that had been called to evaluate Joanna said that she had to be operated on immediately. They took Joanna down the hall to the surgical room but did not return for some time. We became very concerned. Finally the pediatrician, who was a Christian, came back and told us that when they put the needle in to drain the pressure, the soft spot went down on its own and there was no pressure! Joanna had been healed. We took her to the neurosurgeon four months later. After examining her, he said, "Don't ever bring her back. We can't even find scars." Today Joanna is the mother of four children and is happily serving the Lord.

Mrs. Bess Williams
Alvin, Texas

I was born in 1924 and raised in the Alliance Church in East St. Louis, Illinois. When I was two I became very ill. My mom wrapped me in a blanket, got on the trolley car and took me to the parsonage. The pastor, knowing immediately that it was diphtheria, prayed with my mom. I was healed instantly!

When I was four and my brother George was two, mother was expecting another baby. Complications mounted to such a degree that the doctor said an abortion was absolutely necessary or the baby would be physically or mentally disabled. "God has given me this baby, and He will take care of it and me," mother proclaimed. The doctor did not argue with such a woman of great faith. All went smoothly and we had another brother, Bob.

Some time later Bob developed rheumatic fever. At that time the advances of modern medicine were not available. A man came to town and held healing meetings in a tent. I do not recall names or denominations. Mom decided to take Bob to the tent. Since Dad was not a believer, she went alone, carrying the boy in her arms. Later, as I was in the yard with my father, we heard Bob yell, "Hey, guys, look at me!" He was running home as fast as he could. All the pain and swelling in his joints were gone. When Dad saw him running he put his hands on his hips and quietly said, "Now I know there is a God!" I'll never forget that scene as long as I live.

Listo Bell
Jamaica, West Indies

I came to the United States in 1985 in order to create a little better way of life for my family. My dream was to have my husband join me here in the States. Unfortunately, he died suddenly on April 24, 1987.

I worked in Brookhaven, Pennsylvania. It was my practice to pray for protection before I drove off each day and thank God whenever I reached my destination. The morning before my accident was no exception.

That afternoon I had to return to work as I had forgotten some things. Driving down a busy main street in Chester, Pennsylvania, I suddenly blacked out for a few seconds. I didn't know what was happening, but I realized the car was pulling hard to the right. I became frightened and, missing the brake pedal, I stepped on the gas pedal. My car went across an embankment and slammed into a tree at 50 m.p.h.

Before I hit the tree I knew I was in danger and said, "I will now see my husband just eight days before the second anniversary of his death." After I hit the tree I felt my feet become as cold as ice and knew I could not live. I raised my right hand to heaven and prayed, "Lord, have mercy on my soul."

My eyes closed, my head fell backward and I knew nothing more except that breath suddenly left my body. I saw my spirit going upward. It went up . . . up . . . up and then it began to descend, re-entering my body. I became conscious and immediately opened my eyes. My face was hurting so I spat in my hand and found my partial denture was broken in two and all my front teeth had been knocked out. I unhooked my seat belt and opened the door. Experiencing pain all over my body, I just sat there. I began feeling numb and just then a tall white man, about 60 years of age, came up to me and said, "Lady, I was out jogging and I saw everything. Don't move!" Then he touched me and I heard him gasp, "My God, she is bleeding all over."

God was good to me, for although I was traveling on a very busy street, no vehicle was coming nor going when the accident happened. Just as the man (a retired policeman) came to help, other cars came and people began to stop. I heard him say,

"This lady is badly hurt. Call the ambulance. Don't crowd her."

Within seconds the ambulance arrived. The attendants took me out of the car and placed a neck brace on me. Then they placed me in the ambulance, and I heard fear in their voices—my blood pressure was falling.

They rushed me to the hospital trauma unit. The nurses and doctors ran to my side, cut off my clothes and inserted a tube in my mouth to take out some of the blood. They were all doing everything in their power to keep me alive, but all through this I kept saying, "Let me give my children's phone numbers before I lose consciousness." No one understood what I was saying because of my accent and so many broken teeth. Finally an Iranian doctor understood and asked me for the numbers. I gave him two of them. He asked me all the necessary questions. I gave all the answers. He turned to another doctor and exclaimed, "Have you ever seen anyone reel off answers like this in such a condition?!" After 21 X-rays I was placed in intensive care. I vaguely remembered seeing three of my children and friends from the church who had arrived.

My pastor Joe Broz told me he came to pray for me, and the doctors told him to prepare my family because I would not live. Pastor Broze then looked intently into the doctor's eyes, "I didn't come here to bury anybody." His intensity made the doctor freeze in his tracks. Pushing past him, he opened his bottle of anointing oil and arrived at my bedside. Just then I opened my eyes, saw him and said, "Pastor Joe, pray for me." (I remember nothing of this.) He said he anointed me and prayed for me. He then turned back around and told the doctor the Lord had told him I *would* live otherwise. He went out and prayed with my children in the lobby without telling them what the doctor had said. I am not sure if it was the same day, but I know I felt someone touch me.

My right kneecap was broken. My feet were cut badly. There was a problem with my throat. So while the orthopedic doctor was repairing my knee and seeing to the cuts on my feet, another doctor was working on my throat. I am told I spent four hours in the operating room. I remember while I was in ICU a dentist came to extract the teeth that were broken and put some stitches in my mouth without using anesthetic! It hurt badly.

The third day I was taken out of ICU and placed in a room. That same evening an attendant came to take me to the therapy department. As he placed me on the stretcher I saw the attendant, the nurse and two televisions start spinning. I was crying and begging them not to push me over. Then gradually the whole world began to spin— slower and slower—until it stopped. I guess I was reliving the accident.

The third day after I got out of ICU my stomach began to hurt. When my doctor, Dr. Afshari, came to see me he found a very hard lump and sent me for an ultrasound. He discovered I had pancreatitis and placed me on an IV. After several days, my condition was not improving but I was kept alive by prayers and God's amazing grace. Pastor Joe had all The Christian and Missionary Alliance Churches all over the United States praying for me. Other pastors who also knew me had their congregations praying, too. My son who is a pastor in Jamaica had every Christian back there praying. The other six of my nine children called daily from Jamaica and prayed without ceasing.

There were other operations, for I had broken ribs and my liver had been damaged and was decaying—the fluid from it was now penetrating all over my insides. The doctor removed the affected portion and treated the infection, then removed my gall bladder and appendix (right before rupturing!). He also had to make some repairs to my intestines. After this operation I was taken to the recovery room, then to the ICU.

In recovery I listened daily to the Scriptures on cassette tape. Although I could hardly catch my breath, I was now able to sing my own favorite songs: "Hiding in Thee," "Because He Lives" and "Near the Cross."

The accident occurred on April 16, 1989, and I left the hospital May 10, 1989. I never went back for a single therapy session. I rehabilitated myself at home in the bathtub. Today I even walk without a limp.

I look back to when I was in the emergency room and, medically speaking, without hope of surviving, had only minutes to live. I know God did all this for me, not because I am anyone good or special: He healed me for a purpose and for His glory.

God has been so good to me. He is using me to care for needy men and women and has blessed me with a wonderful ministry through my job that allows me to read the Scriptures and pray with those who want me to. My horrendous medical and dental bills have all been either forgiven or paid by friends. I had no medical insurance!

There is neither pen nor paper nor words enough to describe the pain and suffering I went through. I cannot fully explain the experience I had when my life was snatched away from me and then given back. I thank my God for giving me a second chance. The psalmist in chapter 31, verse 15 says, "My times are in your hands." I have decided that:

> Until then, my heart will go on singing
> Until then, with joy I'll carry on
> Until the day my eyes behold that city
> Until the day God calls me home.

I will serve Him until I behold Him face to face, my Savior and my King.

Nancy Persons
Lindale, Texas
(serving as missionary in Bangkok, Thailand)

I was five months pregnant when I went in for a sonogram to find out when Drew was due. I was told that everything was normal. When I followed up at seven months, my doctor asked me if I was sure of the date of conception. Apparently my baby was extremely large. In fact, by the size of him he should have been born by the end of July but I wasn't due until August 23. When Drew was born on August 22, he was a lot bigger than seven and a half pounds—he was 10 pounds! During labor there was meconium in the amniotic fluids, so we needed a couple of neonatal specialists on hand just in case there was a problem with Drew's lungs. This was good because we needed those two doctors plus a nurse to lay across my abdomen in order to push him out. Finally his head crowned, but his shoulders were so huge that his collarbone cracked and broke on the way out.

Once he was out in the open, though, he didn't cry or breathe. They did a full resuscitation with all the necessary equipment and were able to get him to breathe. Drew was immediately rushed to the ICU. The next day I was told that they had performed several X-rays on his neck. I was very worried. Why would they need an X-ray of his neck? They also said that his cry was very unusual. The X-ray showed his esophagus was very, very narrow. The doctors also noted that when he cried he would turn blue, and he had extreme difficulty feeding. In the beginning it could take him two hours to drink four ounces of milk. Every moment was a struggle.

The doctors insisted that we learn infant CPR right away. We were also given a whole new set of rules like we had never heard before; for example:

We could never take a shower if one of us were alone in the house. If we did and the alarm on him went off, no one would ever hear it. Also, there had to be at least two adults in the car with Drew in case there were ever a need to resuscitate him before the driver could pull over. All these rules made us—me especially—very anxious. The alarm (which was hooked to his chest) would go off if he had gone more than 20 seconds without taking a breath. I praise God that the alarm never sounded.

On the second day we had to take him from the hospital in Fairfax, Virginia, to the children's hospital in Washington, DC, to be examined by the heart and lung specialists. After performing a laryngoscopy, they discovered that his vocal cords were paralyzed. We were also told that since this was such a rare occurrence, they had very little information on how he was going to fare as he grew up. There was hope that as his body and organs grew, his airways and esophagus would also grow, but of course, there was no guarantee.

All this was very upsetting as Drew was only four days old. About this time the elders from our church came to pray for Drew. They gathered around his bed in ICU and lifted him up to God. At that same time I was filled with the most wonderful peace and strength. God truly gave me the peace that passes understanding which, by our own efforts, seems so elusive. I would look at the green light blinking and I would think, "He's going to be OK. I don't have to worry about this, he's going to be OK."

I did notice right from the very beginning, though, that whenever I held him he never looked into my eyes; most other babies do. He *did* have a startle reflex which was normal, but if you shook a noisy rattle by the side of his head, he wouldn't turn to look at it. I had mentioned this to my pediatrician a few times but she just brushed it aside saying he was OK. But I knew *something* was wrong. He wasn't smiling or responding as easily as my other baby had.

Finally when he was three months old, we couldn't ignore it any longer; he wasn't following anything with his eyes. Larry and I took him to a specialist and she examined Drew for two hours straight. Finally, we were settled into her office to hear the news. We were told that Drew showed no signs of vision at all. This was strange because his eyes were structurally normal. This indicated that the problem wasn't with his eyes at all—it was in his brain. His brain just wasn't perceiving objects in front of him.

We went home and I totally lost it. Gradually the truth about my son was sinking in deeper and deeper. Larry and I were having a hard time facing the facts. Eventually I got to the point where I questioned what I was going to do, how I would raise a child like him. I was so panic-stricken that my old anxieties returned. I would get short of breath whenever I dwelled too long on Drew and what kind of life he would have.

I had stopped going to my Wednesday evening prayer group because we were so busy with

Drew. However, I received a great deal of support from our church. One woman in particular, was a nurse who was qualified in teaching infant CPR. So she gathered and instructed 11 people in life-saving techniques, just so that I could begin attending church again on a regular basis.

One night I was unusually anxious and asked the ladies to pray for God's help. I wanted either to accept that this was the way things would be or to have God's healing touch on Drew. I expressed to them how completely overwhelmed and drained of strength I was. They all looked rather blasé about it. Finally the leader looked at me and said, "No, I don't think we'll pray for you Nancy. We need to pray for Drew." I sat in a chair and they gathered around me and put their hands on me and prayed, some praying in tongues, some praying in English. When they were finally done praying two women simultaneously said, "My child, it is done." I felt a total release and peace in my heart. I was no longer anxious. I felt everything was completely taken care of.

That night it was my turn to sleep downstairs. Drew woke up at 3:00 a.m. for his bottle, so I rushed around in the dark and began to feed him. I noticed in the dark that Drew seemed to be staring at my face. But since I was so sleepy and groggy, I forgot about the prayer from the night before. I put him back down when we finished and went to sleep.

At 6:00 a.m. he woke up, and as I placed him on my lap to feed he looked right into my eyes! I couldn't believe it! Soon he was asleep and a little later, around 9:00 a.m., he got up again and this time he was definitely looking into my eyes. I laid him on the floor, took a rattle and passed it in front of his eyes. Left-right, right-left. I took it to the side of his head and shook it on either side. Drew turned his head both ways. He just lay there smiling and cooing. I ran to the phone and called Larry and told him everything that had happened. I kept screaming, "Drew's OK! Drew's OK! He can see!" I was totally psyched and excited! I laid Drew back on the floor and throughout the rest of the day he rolled over five times (something which he had never done before).

After Larry came home and we talked about it, I expressed to him that I was sure his vocal cords were healed as well. We decided to take him back the next day to the children's hospital to have him examined. The doctors were surprised because they had only seen him two weeks prior. They said that his vocal cords were fine! Both sides were vibrating naturally. I tried explaining everything to the doctors about the prayer, but they were very skeptical. The doctors had no belief that a miracle had taken place.

All this occurred around Thanksgiving—so the day after we had him dedicated to God. It was a wonderful time for everyone because we had so much to be thankful for. Drew seemed to be delayed socially about three months, behind all the other healthy babies. This was, of course, totally natural since everything was a brand-new experience of sight and sound for him. But after he reached a year, he was completely caught up.

No matter where we go or what country we are in, everyone either comments on how beautiful his eyes are or how far his voice carries. And I have realized that these words are the Lord's gentle reminder to me, "Remember, I did this for Drew. I gave him his sight. I gave him his voice." The miracle became a wonderful witness to friends, Christian and non-Christian alike. I wrote everyone, telling them everything that had happened and praising God for what He had done. How could anyone live without God? How do people face crises without Him? He is so faithful! Look at what He's done for us! Look at what He's done for Drew!

Elaine Enos
Sunnyvale, California

In January 1993 I was diagnosed with an inoperable brain tumor. It was in an area the doctors could not reach, causing terrible pain and visual problems. I cried out to God, and He immediately removed all the fear and despair that had overcome me. An overwhelming peace replaced my uncertainties; I sensed that He would heal me one way or the other. Peace and faith never left me. Through my daughter, I was given the Scripture Isaiah 61:1, 3:

> The Spirit of the Sovereign LORD is on me, because the LORD has anointed me . . . to be-

stow on them . . . the oil of gladness instead of mourning, and a garment of praise instead of a spirit of despair. They will be called oaks of righteousness, a planting of the LORD for the display of his splendor.

God brought about His will in order that splendor would be His. Prayers and support of several different groups of people had a direct impact on my recovery. I underwent an arteriogram, a procedure in which the doctor threads a tiny catheter through an artery in the leg, up through the body, heart and into the brain. Then he injects a dye and takes X-rays. At one point, the catheter hit a snag in the artery in my neck and would not slip through. I felt the doctor pushing and pushing, and I was getting more and more tense and concerned, which didn't help! I turned to God and remembered someone praying for me the previous night, quoting Isaiah 53:5: "By his wounds we are healed." I asked Jesus to take away my tension and anxiety. Instantly the Holy Spirit's calmness and relaxation swept over me and I heard the doctor breathe a sigh of relief as the catheter slipped through.

In February, a four-hour surgery was scheduled to obtain a needle biopsy in order to diagnose the tumor. When the doctors operated, they found that about one-third of the tumor was growing out into an area they could cut and burn off, thus blocking the blood supply to the rest of the tumor left inside—a direct answer to prayer.

A month after surgery the MRI showed the tumor shrinking. My right eye, however, was worse. I was unable to use it at all. But the awful headaches were gone and I praised God.

After recovering from surgery and six weeks of radiation therapy, I flew up to Washington to help our son and his wife move and take care of their baby. We worked hard, packing, cleaning and loading the trucks. I was designated to drive the pickup on ahead with the baby and try to get to the house before dark so I could put the baby to bed. Off I went.

However, the pickup was loaded beyond capacity and I couldn't see out the rear-view mirror. The driver's side mirror was broken from a minor accident and was unusable. It was dusk, and I was dead tired, driving 90 miles on roads I had never driven before, some under construction, searching for the right turn-offs to three different freeways and a long narrow road to a little house on a lake . . . with one eye! It was difficult and stressful. Again I called out to God. In fact, I was praying all the way. I covered all bases, not only asking Him to get us there safely, but pleading with Him to have mercy on me and heal my eye because I needed it so badly and I knew He was able. Psalm 120:1 is a verse I now claim, "I call on the LORD in my distress, and he answers me."

I made it safely to the house and got myself and the baby to bed. The next morning when I got up, my eyesight was perfect. The right eye lined up perfectly with the left. When I returned home and saw the eye surgeon, who had been in on my case since the beginning, she was amazed and couldn't believe it! She said she had planned to operate and move the muscles in an attempt to ease the problem. God not only healed my vision that day but He gave me a deeper respect and awe for His power and sovereignty and a new sense that He is in charge and can do anything! He knows everything that is going on in the world and will do what is best for us when it brings about a display of His splendor.

In recent years God also healed my husband who had gone deaf in one ear during military service in Korea. God had laid it on someone else's heart to pray for us. We had thought we were just supposed to live with his condition. But one day someone stopped us in the sanctuary of the church we were visiting that Sunday. He said, "You are deaf in your left ear aren't you?" We were puzzled. We didn't even know the man! He continued. "The Lord Jesus wants to restore you today." We submitted to his words and prayed with him. When he finished, my husband Warren put his watch to his deaf ear. We were not prepared for the joy in the Holy Spirit that has followed us from that moment to now. Warren burst out, "Honey, I can hear again!"

That incident began a tremendous change in our lives, marriage and family. We've never been the same. We serve an awesome, loving (and surprising!) God.

Bill Myers
Fort Collins, Colorado (Alliance Evangelical Church)

I had gone to a nearby ranch to deliver bad news to one of our elders—there were complications with his daughter's pregnancy and she was being rushed in for an emergency caesarean section. Our church's prayer chain was activated and we waited for further news. The initial news was great. The surgery, rushed though it had been, was entirely successful and mother and child were doing well. It was early the next morning when I first heard the concerns the doctor had about a lump that had appeared under the child's jaw, but also a combination of perilous blood abnormalities. During the next two days, waiting for test results, the rapid decline of the infant's health had everyone alarmed.

As the elders and I answered the parent's call and drove to the hospital, my concern was how to comfort these young parents, recently renewed in their faith, who would soon face the loss of their first child. Even as the elders and I prayed in a small waiting room down the hall from obstetrics, I was searching for the right words to say to explain God's actions in robbing them of this joy.

When I walked into that hospital room, saw the faces of this family I loved, God spoke very clearly to my heart. His words were, "Tell me, Bill, why do you think this child should die?" Trembling at my Lord's rebuke, I prayed with a faith for that touch, that healing, that I had never known before. (Even now . . . writing these words, trying vainly to describe the sense of God's undeniable promise to those people at that time, in that place, for that healing . . . my eyes are filled with tears.) I prayed words that were not mine nor do I recollect them—words that a compassionate Father wanted delivered to a pair of His children that afternoon. It was a powerful moment.

Before we arrived that afternoon, the doctors had made the decision to transport the infant to a larger medical center before his condition could further deteriorate. Their concern was deepened by the fact that after our prayer with him and his parents, he slept for the first time since his birth. He received no other treatment before being whisked away. The experts examined, tested and X-rayed. Early the next morning the young father's voice was on the other end of the phone: "They said they can't imagine what the people down there were thinking about. They want to know why our hospital sent them this healthy baby."

The blood abnormalities had been corrected. The lump beneath his little jaw, thought to be a thyroid tumor, was nearly invisible by ultrasound the next day. He was held for observation and released to his parents. He is one of the biggest, healthiest, happiest little boys I've known. Jesus reigns, He saves and He heals.

Chuck Davis
*Christian and Missionary Alliance Missionary
in Bamako, Mali, Africa*
We witnessed a tremendous healing while serv-

ing in New Jersey prior to being sent to France for language study. A young family had experienced new life in Christ. Part of His redemptive work in their lives was to miraculously save their marriage. Several times the wife had packed her suitcase to leave, but each time the Lord intervened.

In the spring of 1988, their new experiences of God's victory caused them to have unlimited faith in the Lord. During this time, their three-year-old son broke his leg. They had the break confirmed through emergency room X-rays and the leg was set in a cast. The father was not satisfied with this intervention because of hearing a series of messages on divine healing at his church. He called the pastor and asked him to pray for the complete healing of his son. In faith, he returned to the doctor to have the leg re-examined. The second set of X-rays showed no sign of the break. Another X-ray was taken, confirming the results. The doctor was amazed and could not explain it . . . that was the first time he had *ever* cut off a new cast within 48 hours of applying it!

Later, we were in the midst of language study in France, a daily 10-hour regimen of intense study. During this time, we experienced many attacks from the enemy. One such attack occurred when Ingrid, my wife, developed a severe neck problem. The pain became so intense that she could not remain in class nor give herself to her studies. We discerned this was a physical attack from the enemy to discourage us and to hamper our missionary training.

Before leaving America, Ingrid had experienced many back and neck adjustments by chiropractors. We were concerned about going to France, as most French chiropractors used New Age principles of healing which we interpreted as dangerous and demonic. We were also concerned because our destination was Mali, West Africa, where chiropractors could not be found. With this problem, we sensed that Ingrid would not be able to continue.

During a Sunday evening worship service, organized to encourage us missionaries studying French, we set aside a time for people to come to the front for prayer. That night we gathered around Ingrid, laid hands on her, binding the spirits who desired to torment her and invited the Lord to divinely intervene. During the prayer time she experienced a warm sensation in her neck. We accepted it as the Lord's intervention. She has not been restricted from working because of neck pain since.

Lynn Conat
Kalispell, Montana

After a week's hospital stay in 1973 I was diagnosed with multiple sclerosis. I was not informed I had MS; I was only told I had a virus. I always knew that something was wrong but could never pinpoint the trouble. (I did not know Jesus Christ as my Lord and Savior.)

In 1991 I went blind in my right eye. After several months of numerous medical tests, including an MRI (brain scan), I was diagnosed with optical neuritis. It was caused by the MS. The shock was terrific, but by this time my husband and I had come to the Lord. We knew where to go for strength and guidance. Soon I began to feel an incredible peace and saw God's protective hand on me even back when I didn't know Him. I would not have been able to handle the truth about my MS condition had I known about it back in 1973. God, in His mercy, waited until I knew Him and was able to handle such news.

My vision slowly returned, but by the following winter I had another attack of optic neuritis and went blind for the second time. It was a very painful condition, yet God was right by my side once again, enabling me to sleep without pain. During this time my medical records were sent up from California and the MS diagnosis was revealed. Despite the slow return of my vision, there was permanent damage to my right eye. Nothing could be done to improve the dark film over it. God drew me closer to Him, to a sweet dependence on His unfailing love. I began to have trouble with my arms and hands—weakness, numbness and pain. I also had nerve damage in my leg from the first attack. My greatest battle was with fatigue and total exhaustion.

Despite being anointed and prayed over several times, nothing changed, including my peace about the situation. When I heard about the healing service at Riverside Alliance I had no intention of attending. I saw Mike Phillips a few days before the service and he insisted that I attend. At the conclusion of the service, I came forward for healing, resting in whatever decision God would make. When I was being prayed for I felt overwhelmed, and I could only repeat Jesus' name over and over. When the spirit of infirmity was bound and commanded to leave my body, I felt the weight of the fatigue lift. When I opened my eyes, Reverend Bill Putnam stared straight at me, saying, "This is a complete healing, and in the morning you will know it." It was true God had chosen that service to heal me. The next morning the dark film had been removed and my eyes were normal and completely clear. *Praise God!* Not once since then have I experienced any MS symptoms. My hands and arms are strong with no numbness and my left leg is strong after being damaged for 21 years. My energy level is amazing, especially to my husband.

Local Church Healing Ministries

We see the work God is doing in people today as a testimony to His lovingkindness. And yet God is not just doing His work in isolated individual cases. He is using churches and giving them thriving healing ministries as they pray and plan to minister the whole Word of God to the lost (and the saved!) who need God's therapeutic, saving touch. Here are some of their stories.

While some churches have abandoned the practice of healing, other congregations are experiencing a renewal of this work for Christ. These churches see scores of people healed in the name of our Lord Jesus Christ each year.

Pastoral involvement is a key to a vital healing ministry in the local church. When the pastor is convinced that Christ still heals today that conviction will be reflected in his preaching. He will also take time to train the lay-elders in the theology of divine healing and in the actual practice of healing. Like A.B. Simpson these pastors do not view healing as a fringe issue. They understand it to be a gospel blessing accompanied by vital evangelism and personal growth in holiness. The exaltation of Christ our Healer is a necessary component in the worship and practice of a healthy Christian assembly.

The following accounts of local church healing ministries show divine healing to be alive and well at the end of the 20th century. This blessing is for today.

Allegheny Center Alliance Church
Pittsburgh, PA

This congregation founded by E.D. Whiteside over a century ago has in recent years enjoyed a revival of healing comparable to the early days of this great work. Pastor Rockwell Dillaman affirms evident manifestation of God's power to heal the sick in the congregational life of Allegheny Center Church. He attributes this blessing to the consistent preaching on healing and the participation of the elders in this ministry.

Elders are at the altar prepared to pray for the sick at every service.

The pastor observes three aspects of the healing ministry of their church. Anointing with oil, the laying on of hands and prayer are regularly practiced in the church's ministry to the sick. Often persons are healed before they can be anointed with oil. Such healing takes place during times of intense worship and praise to the Lord. The exaltation of Christ in these times of praise quickens the faith of some resulting in instantaneous healing. Times of prayers for those bound by evil spirits have resulted in some remarkable healing. During one such session of spiritual warfare praying, a lady who had suffered seven years with phlebitis was completely healed. She had also been afflicted with hemorrhages. This condition was healed at the same time.

This historic church does not see divine healing as a relic of the past but a reality for now. Instead of dying as many such churches are doing, Allegheny Center Alliance Church is a growing, active congregation in the central city of one of America's great metropolitan areas. Their vital healing ministry is an integral part of their outreach to needy people of all races and social classes in the greater Pittsburgh area.

First Alliance Church
Lexington, KY
The First Alliance Church in Lexington, Kentucky is a growing church with a dynamic outreach

to its community. The congregation is composed of professionals, college and university students and professors, physicians, middle-management people, plus people from all walks of life. Pastor Ron Gifford is excited about the renewal of the ministry of divine healing going on in their midst.

It began with the elders of the church. At a weekend retreat the elders became convinced that they needed to take seriously their responsibility to biblically carry out the ministry of divine healing. During the months that followed, these elders studied, prayed and sometimes fasted in preparation for an effective ministry of healing to their church. As time went by the intercession of the elders and pastoral staff was heard. Marvelous incidents of healing began to occur.

Over time there developed the concept of healing as a vital part of pastoral care. While opportunities are given for anointing with oil and prayer in the public services and at the monthly communion services, much of the healing ministry is initiated as members relate to their elders. The elders have so developed their gifts and sensitivity as to be able to inspire faith for healing and to relate healing to the spiritual needs of the members who approach them. The results of this method have been phenomenal.

The success of this approach to healing has created a whole new level of trust in the congregation. Members feel free to go to the elders for prayer and counseling when they have physical need. The compassion and active faith of these dedicated elders is conducive to presenting Christ as Healer. Their biblical understanding of this gospel truth equips them with insight and discernment that really helps the seeker meet Christ the Healer. The spiritual aspects of the seeker's condition are not overlooked but wisely dealt with by the elders.

The testimonies of extraordinary healings are making an impact on the whole church. Pastor Gifford says that a side effect of the revitalizing of divine healing has been the spiritual renewal among the elders engaged in this work. So many outstanding healings have taken place that an effort is now in progress to compile a book of these up-to-date testimonies of physical healings.

Hillside Chapel Alliance Church
Dayton, OH

Some 17 years ago a small Alliance Church in Dayton was led of the Lord to relocate in Beavercreek, a growing suburb of Dayton, Ohio. From the beginning this congregation began to grow and experience the blessing that comes from the preaching of the fullness of Christ. Pastor Nelson says that divine healing has been a part of the ministry throughout the last 17 years. During the early years of this ministry, member of the church was diagnosed by medical doctors as having terminal cancer. After anointing and prayer, Mark Young was healed and is still a healthy and active member of Hillside Chapel. As the church increased in size, Pastor Nelson found it necessary to devote some of his messages to healing in order to instruct the newcomers and the new converts on the doctrine of healing. Consistent instruction has been a part of the methodology used in the Hillside Chapel healing ministry.

The elders are taught and trained to carry on a healing ministry. The church, in addition to its public healing ministry, often goes to hospitals or homes to pray for the sick. At every communion service there is anointing and prayer for those suffering physical needs. At the Sunday evening services, testimonies of healing are often heard as people tell of God's healing touch on their lives. During the interview for this article, the pastor shared his personal testimony. Recently after anointing and prayer he was definitely healed of a serious back problem.

Another active healing ministry at Hillside Chapel is the deliverance of those bound or possessed by demons. Some of the elders devote time to dealing with these cases. Just as Jesus and the apostolic church cast out demons so Hillside Chapel takes this ministry as an essential part of the ministry of healing. Regularly this congregation continues to see people who are bound by the powers of darkness set free.

Hillside Chapel continues to grow. They are in the midst of another major building project. The preaching and practice of the Fourfold Gospel is at the heart of this church's ministry. Divine healing is a norm in the life of Hillside Chapel.

Eagle Alliance Church
Indianapolis, IN

Healing is happening not only in older and well-established churches but also in new extension churches. The Eagle Alliance Church in Indianapolis, Indiana, is four years old and already has a regular attendance of 400. Kerry Bowman, the pastor of this young and growing church, is convinced that physical healing in answer to prayer is for today. From the beginning he has conducted a praise and ministry service designed to instruct the congregation in deeper truths including divine healing and the ministry of deliverance.

The church has developed a successful small group ministry. One such group is composed of people with a great burden for intercession. Here people are trained to pray for the bound and for others with physical needs. From this small group comes people who assist the pastor in a very vital ministry of deliverance. A strong group of intercessors also undergird the deliverance team.

Divine healing is a public ministry in Eagle Alliance Church. Their monthly communion services are conducted on Sunday evenings and always include anointing and prayer for the sick. The teaching of Christ as Healer is a new concept to many who have come to this extension congregation making teaching and the actual practice of this truth essential. A medical doctor who recently came to the Eagle Alliance Church was quite skeptical about divine healing until she saw a miracle of healing. A boy in the church was diagnosed as having a brain tumor with little, if any, hope for recovery. After anointing and prayer he was completely healed. It is exciting to see how the blessed truth of Christ as Healer is an important factor in the growth and spiritual health of this recently formed church. The work of the Eternal Christ in healing the sick and loosing those who have been bound is a reality in the life of Eagle Alliance Church.

Elberta Alliance Church
Elberta, AL

Pastor Donald Young and a layman from his church had no idea of the results of a trip to visit and minister in the Alliance churches of Chile. In the midst of their excitement at visiting a mission field, God poured out His Spirit in an unusual measure upon these visitors and the Chilean church. Not only were people saved and filled with the Spirit in large numbers, but the Lord was also pleased to heal the sick and set free the bound. Glorious days of revival followed the initial outpouring. It was a life-changing experience for these men. They laid hands on the blind who were then made to see. Miracles became the order of the day. In awe this pastor and his elders stood back and watched the hand of God work on a level with the book of Acts. The leadership of the Chilean church wept for joy. It was a never-to-be-forgotten, life-changing experience for all who were there.

For the next chapter of this story one must go to Elberta, Alabama, the location of Donald

Young's church. The Lord had been blessing the Elberta congregation with new life and growth but now a new era was about to begin. As the men came back home from Chile, they were pondering the revival they had just experienced and wondered if God could do a work like that in Elberta, Alabama. The answer to that question came very soon. The first Sunday back, as the congregation gathered to hear the report from Pastor Young and the elder who went with him to Chile, a mighty wind of revival began to blow. The same glorious work they witnessed in Chile occurred in the Elberta church. Souls were saved, believers were filled with the Spirit, the sick were healed and demons were cast out in Christ's name.

The moving of the Holy Spirit on this church brought them deep spiritual change and a revitalization of the ministry of healing unlike anything the church had previously known. How marvelous are the works of God. He still confirms His gospel by the supernatural healing of the sick and the exorcism of evil spirits in Christ's name. Revival is obviously the key to the renewal of healing in this church.

Conclusion

The above ministries and stories are convincing testimonies to God's healing power today. People in these stories simply read the Bible and trusted God's Word as the true guide for their lives.

Are we going to live out a half-baked gospel? We cannot shrink to that. We must obey our

Lord and heal the sick because the gospel is a gospel of power. Luke 5:17ff shows that Jesus has the power to forgive and the power to heal. This means healing is part of the gospel message. Though healing does not always accompany salvation, salvation always changes people. The change is never exclusively spiritual, just as healing is never exclusively physical. God wants us involved in experiencing healing and training people in the whole counsel of God.

We must heal the sick also because we serve a Savior who healed the sick. And if we live for Jesus, then we are to advance His kingdom. Yes, there will be "failures" as we launch out in obedience. But the Scriptures say, "[F]or though a righteous man falls down seven times, he rises again" (Proverbs 24:16a).

We must be mindful that God's will needs to become our will too. The Holy Spirit has an agenda to bind up the wounded, to heal the brokenhearted, to preach good news to the poor, to proclaim freedom for the prisoners and recovery of sight for the blind, to release the oppressed, to comfort those who mourn, to heal the sick, lame and blind, to preach the gospel of Jesus Christ to every creature, to baptize them as a testimony of their new life and make disciples in every nation. This is God's will. Let's do it and hasten His coming!

Summary of Hebrew Words, Old Testament References

Hebrew Words

Rapha—heal, sew together, mend, remedy; refers to general correction.

Marpe—cure, healing, health (almost equivalent to *rapha*).

Te-alah—the physical process of the healing of new flesh over a wound; stopping the flow of blood.

Arukhah—the growth of new flesh at the wounded spot; refers to extending out.

Kehah—alleviation; refers to taking away or removing (such as a malady).

Subh—restore, return (from bad to good again); refers to bringing back.

Alah—go up, bring up; refers to filling up.

Qum—arise, stand.

Hayah—revive, "quicken"; refers to putting (life) in.

Hadash—renew, repair, make anew, start over.

Halaph—renew, sprout anew.

See page 218 for an illustrated description of the Hebrew words for healing.

Selected Incidents and Statements Regarding Healing in the Old Testament

Genesis 20:17: God heals Abimelech. His wife and slave girls' wombs "opened" again.

Genesis 21:1-2: Sarah becomes pregnant at around 91 years old.

Genesis 25:21: The barren Rebekah becomes pregnant.

Genesis 29:30-31: Leah's womb is opened.

Genesis 30-22-23: Rachel's womb opened and she bears Joseph.

Exodus 4:6-7: Moses' hand made leprous and restored.

Exodus 15:22-26: Water is cured and God makes the statement.

Exodus 23:25-26: They will be exempt from many illnesses if they worship the LORD.

Numbers 12:9-16: Miriam's leprosy is healed.

Numbers 16:46-50: The plague is stopped.

Numbers 21:4-9: Israelites are healed from snakebites.

Deuteronomy 28:15-68: Failed health is a major part of the threat regarding disobedience.

Deuteronomy 32:39: "I have wounded and I will heal."

1 Samuel 6:3: The Philistines are offered healing if they return the ark.

1 King 13:1-6: Jeroboam's hand withered and restored.

1 Kings 17:8-24: Widow's son raised from dead.

2 Kings 2:19-22: Well water at Jericho healed.

2 Kings 4:8-36: Shunnamite family blessed with a son (vv. 15-17), raised from dead (vv. 32-35).

2 Kings 5:1-19: Naaman cleansed of leprosy.

2 King 6:8-23: Eyesight blinded and restored to Arameans.

2 Kings 13:21: Dead man comes to life in Elisha's tomb.

2 Kings 20:1-11: God promises and Hezekiah is healed.

2 Chronicles 7:14: Conditions for forgiveness and healing of the land are stated.

2 Chronicles 30:20: God heals at Hezekiah's petition.

Job 5:18: "He injures, but his hands also heal."

Psalm 30:2: "I called to you for help and you healed me."

Psalm 103:2-3: "Praise the LORD . . . who heals your diseases."

Psalm 105:37: "[A]nd from among their tribes no one faltered."

Psalm 107:20: "He sent forth his word and healed them."

Proverbs 12:18: "[T]he tongue of the wise brings healing."

Proverbs 13:17: "[A] trustworthy envoy brings healing."

Proverbs 15:4: "The tongue that brings healing is a tree of life."

Proverbs 16:24: "Pleasant words are . . . healing to the bones."

Isaiah 19:22: After striking he will heal them. (Egypt).

Isaiah 33:24: No one in Zion will say "I am ill."

Isaiah 35:5-6: Blind, deaf, lame and mute are cured.

Isaiah 42:1 & 7: God's servant will open blind eyes.

Isaiah 53:5: "[B]y *his* wounds we are healed. (emphasis added)"

Isaiah 57:18-19: "I will heal him; . . . I will heal them."

Isaiah 58:8: "[Y]our healing will quickly appear."

Jeremiah 30:17: "I will restore you to health and heal your wounds."

Jeremiah 33:6: "I will heal my people."

Ezekiel 47:12: "[T]heir leaves (will be) for healing."

Daniel 3:19-27: Fire does not burn Daniel and his friends.

Daniel 4:34: Nebuchadnezzar's sanity is restored.

Hosea 6:1: "[T]he LORD . . . he will heal us."

Hosea 11:3: "[I]t was I who healed them."

Hosea 14:4: "I will heal their waywardness."

Jonah 2:10: Jonah is preserved.

Malachi 4:2: "[T]he sun of righteousness will rise with healing in its wings."

Jesus' Works of Healing

The Healing: Distinction and Method

References

1. The unclean spirit/demon is hushed and cast out of a man by Jesus' speaking (Mark 1:23-28; Luke 4:33-37).

2. Peter's mother-in-law's fever healed by Jesus' rebuke and touch (Matthew 8:14-15; Mark 1:29-31; Luke 4:38-39).

3. Jesus healed many who were brought to Him of sickness and demonization by a word and touch (Matthew 8:16-17; Mark 1:32-34; Luke 4:40-41).

4. Jesus preaches and casts out many demons (Mark 1:39).

5. A leper comes to Jesus in faith; Jesus has compassion, touches him and pronounces him clean; he is healed (Matthew 8:1-4; Mark 1:40-45; Luke 5:12-16).

6. Bed-ridden paralytic is brought to Jesus; Jesus speaks forgiveness and healing to him (Matthew 9:1-8; Mark 2:1-12; Luke 5:17-26).

7. Jesus commands the man with a shriveled hand and raises it to restoration (Matthew 12:9-14; Mark 3:1-6; Luke 6:6-11).

8. Many come to touch Jesus; He heals all of disease and unclean spirits *(Scholars are not settled regarding the distinction between this multitude-healing and #23 below). (Matthew 12:15-16; Mark 3:7-12).

9. Jesus speaks to drive the demons out of the Gerasene demoniac(s) (Matthew says there were two) (Matthew 8:28-34; Mark 5:1-20; Luke 8:26-39).

10. Jesus' touch and command to rise heals Jairus' dying daughter (Matthew 9:18-19, 23-26; Mark 5:21-24, 35-43; Luke 8:40-42, 49-56).

11. Woman touches Jesus in faith and is healed of 12 years of hemorrhaging (Matthew 9:20-22; Mark 5:25-34; Luke 8:43-48.)

12. Jesus heals a few in Nazareth; activity is limited by unbelief (Matthew 13:58; Mark 6:5-6).

13. All brought to Him in Gennesaret are healed by touching His garment (Matthew 14:34-36; Mark 6:53-56).

14. Canaanite woman's faith and plea have Jesus cast a demon from her daughter (Matthew 15:21-28; Mark 7:24-30).

15. Jesus heals a deaf/mute by touch, saliva and speaking (Mark 7:31-37).

16. A blind man is brought to Jesus in Bethsaida; He heals him with saliva and by touching him (Mark 8:22-26).

17. At the father's request Jesus liberates a demonized boy by rebuking the spirit and lifting the boy (Matthew 17:14-21; Mark 9:14-29; Luke 9:37-43a).

18. Through faith, blind Bartimaeus receives sight; Jesus has compassion, touches him and speaks healing (Matthew differs by referring to two men and saying this healing happened while leaving Jericho [see Mark and Luke] (Matthew 20:29-34; Mark 10:46-52; Luke 18:35-43).

19. Jesus heals a centurion's servant by the centurion's request in faith (Luke says elders and friends implored of Jesus) (Matthew 8:5-13; Luke 7:1-10).

20. Two blind men in Galilee request in faith and receive sight via Jesus' touch (Matthew 9:27-31).

21. Jesus casts demon from a mute man and his speech returns (Matthew 9:32-34).

22. Jesus heals a demonized man, blind and mute (Luke only mentions mute) (Matthew 12:22-24; Luke 11:14-15).

23. At Galilee Jesus preaches, teaches and heals every disease in people from Galilee, Syria, Judea etc. (Scholars are not settled regarding

the distinction between this multitude-healing and #8 above) (Matthew 4:23-25; Luke 6:17-19)

24. Jesus is moved with compassion; He heals every sickness and disease (Matthew 9:35-36)

25. Jesus heals many of many things and says, "[R]eport to John" (Matthew 11:2-6; Luke 7:18-23).

26. In Galilee Jesus has compassion and heals those who are in need (Matthew 14:14; Luke 9:11; John 6:2).

27. Jesus heals great multitudes in Galilee: The lame, maimed, blind, etc. (Matthew 15:29-31).

28. Leaving Galilee Jesus heals many in Judea beyond the Jordan (Matthew 19:1-2).

29. The blind and lame came to Jesus in the temple and He healed them (Matthew 21:14).

30. Jesus has compassion and raises the widow's dead son by speaking to him (Luke 7:11-17).

31. Jesus had cast seven demons out of Mary Magdalene (Luke 8:2).

32. Jesus heals the woman with the bent back by speaking to and touching her (Luke 13:10-13ff).

33. Jesus touches and heals a man with dropsy (Luke 14:1-4).

34. Jesus speaks and 10 lepers are healed (faith is also a factor) (Luke 17:11-19).

35. Jesus touches the High Priest's servant's ear and it is restored (Luke 22:49-51).

36. Great multitudes gather near Jesus to hear and be healed (Luke 5:15).

37. Jesus casts out demons and cures people (Tell Herod!) (Luke 13:32).

38. Jesus speaks and an official from Capernaum has faith; his son lives (John 4:46-53).

39. Jesus speaks and a man lame for 38 years walks again (John 5:1-9).

40. By anointing with saliva-clay and giving a command, Jesus heals a man born blind (John 9:1-11).

41. Jesus has compassion and speaks to raise Lazarus from the dead (John 11:1-44).

This panoramic chart of Jesus' healing ministry is what is referred to throughout Part II, "Healing in the Time of Jesus." It is adapted from the one found in *Power Healing*, entitled "Overview of the Healing Ministry of Jesus," pp. 245-246. Some of the references have been expanded to contain crucial information prior to or following a healing. This way the fundamental compulsion for doing the healing and the reaction following the healing are included.

The sequence of the healings found in *Power Healing* is maintained. Students of the New Testament realize that the healings of Jesus are not presented in the same order in each of the gospels. This is a topic of much discussion/debate within scholastic circles doing form criticism. However, since form criticism is not within the purpose of this book, it is simpler to follow the order set forth in *Power Healing*.

Mark's Gospel provides the order that the healings are in. Scholars call this the "Marcan spine." This sequence is maintained up through healing #18 involving blind Bartimaeus (Mark 10:46ff). From there the order alternates between Matthew and Luke. The final healings listed are from John's Gospel, for John has several healings that are unique to his account.

Survey of Alliance Leaders

The following is an original project; a survey
was administered twice to roughly 100 Alliance leaders. Its purpose was to check the current
belief and practice of divine healing in The Christian and Missionary Alliance. The first time the
survey was done was in 1989. It was re-administered in 1994 to detect any changes and trends
that were taking place in our beliefs about divine
healing. Thirty missionaries, 30 pastors and all Alliance college and seminary professors of Bible
and theology in the USA participated in the survey. (There were 37 professors in 1989 and 42 in
1994.)

The process for choosing the 30 missionaries
was as follows: Each missionary furloughing in
the United States as of spring 1989 and 1994 (a
random selection in itself) was given a number
and entered into a computer at Alliance Theological Seminary. The computer picked 30 at random.
For the USA pastors, all 2,600 plus were given a
number and that number was again entered into

the computer. The computer again chose 30 at random. With the professors, however, it was important to be inclusive. With their comprehensive number at 37 (and 42 in 1994) it was possible to survey each one. All surveys were conducted by means of a phone call averaging 15-20 minutes.

Below are the formats and results of the surveys:

PASTORAL SURVEY

Name: _____

Age:_____Gender: _____

Education Level _____

Name of school(s): _____

_____

_____

_____

Where ministering:

_____

Years there?_____

How long have you been a minister?_____

Ministered outside CMA? n_____y_____

With whom? _____

1. What does the term "divine healing" bring to mind?

_____

2. Have you yourself experienced divine healing?
n___ y___ If "yes" describe briefly:

_____

_____

3. Have you observed a divine healing? n___ y___
If "yes" describe briefly:

_____

4. Have you been involved in the ministry of divine healing? n___ y___ If "yes" describe briefly:

_____

5. What books would you recommend on the subject?

_____

_____

(The missionary survey differed only slightly, the distinction being in the format of the preliminary questions.)

MISSIONARY SURVEY

Name: _____

Age:_____ Gender: _____

Education level: _____

Name of school(s): _____

_____

_____

_____

Where serving: _____

Years there?_____

Other country(s)? n___ y___

Where and how long?

_____

Served outside CMA? n___ y___ With whom?

_____

1. What does the term "divine healing" bring to mind?

_____

2. Have you yourself experienced divine healing? n___ y___ If "yes" describe briefly:

_____

3. Have you observed divine healing? n___y___

If "yes" describe briefly:

_____

4. Have you been involved in the ministry of divine healing? n___y___ If "yes" describe briefly:

_____

5. What books would you recommend on the subject?

_____

(The survey for educators was also unique in its preliminary tailoring. But more important, the inserted questions 5, 6 and 7 were added because of the unique position these educators have in that they are shaping the minds of future Alliance leaders.)

EDUCATOR SURVEY

Name: _____

Age:_____Gender: _____

Education Level:_____

Years there: _____

Subject(s) taught: _____

Degrees earned & schools attended:

_____

_____

Taught outside CMA? n___y___ With whom?

_____

1. What does the term "divine healing" bring to mind?

_____

2. Have you yourself experienced divine healing? n___y___ If "yes" describe briefly:

_____

3. Have you observed a divine healing? n___y___ If "yes" describe briefly:

_____

4. Have you been involved in the ministry of divine healing? n___ y___ If "yes" describe briefly:

_____

5. Do you teach divine healing? n___ y___ Please comment:

_____

6. Is divine healing in the formal curriculum that you use?

_____

7. What is your stated position on divine healing?

_____

_____

_____

8. What books would you recommend on the subject?

_____

_____

_____

SURVEY RESULTS

(The answers are tallied and set in graphic layout for ease of analysis.)

People answered in one of three ways: In the first division are those who are very absolute about divine healing. They see it as a reality from God for us today. These I categorize as "positive." Among those who were positive, there were seven certain themes that people spoke in terms of: "God's power," "a dynamic experience," "the need to obey God and heal people," "a truth they had learned," "healing in Christ," "a gift from God." The remainder gave no distinction but were certain about God's healing.

Second, there were those who responded favorably but with moderation. They spoke either in terms of God's ability to heal or they had a nondescript notion about divine intervention.

The third category were those who were skeptical about healing. There emerged two types who were skeptical. Either they were rational about the possibility and had their doubts or they felt that healing was for another era in history.

The graphic layout of question one, "What does the term 'divine healing' bring to mind?" is as follows:

(The first number in each box is from the 1989 survey. The number after the slash is from the 1994 survey.)

Question 1. What does the term "divine healing" bring to mind? _____

_____

M=Missionary, P=Pastor, E= Educator

	M	P	E	TOT
VERY POSITIVE ANSWER	20/18	27/16	25/17	72/51
"It is a power from God"	2/6	7/14	4/4	13/24
"It is a dynamic experience"	8/2	7/1	5/1	20/4
"We must be obedient and pray for healing"	5/-	3/1	7/2	15/3
"It is a truth I have learned"	3/-	1/-	-/1	4/1
"There is healing in Christ"	-/6	-/-	4/4	4/10
"It is a gift from God"	-/4	3/-	2/2	5/6

	M	P	E	TOT
No distinct summary, just that it is very positive	2/-	10/-	3/3	15/3
FAVORABLE ANSWER	9/12	3/12	9/22	21/46
"God has the ability"	5/16	3/9	5/17	13/42
"When God intervenes . . ."	4/6	-/3	4/5	8/14

NEGATIVE ANSWER	1/-	-/2	3/3	4/5
(Rational viewpoint)	1/-	-/2	-/3	1/5
(Dispensational viewpoint)	-/-	-/-	3/-	3/-

Question 2. *Have you yourself experienced divine healing? n___ y___ . If "yes" describe briefly.*

_____

_____

(The results, including a comprehensive listing of what they have been healed from, are as follows)

	M	P	E	TOT YES
"YES"	21/22	18/20	18/19	57/61
Below are the details of those who responded "Yes"				
Major sicknesses, such as:				
an internal disease such as terminal cancer	3/-	1/1	-/-	4/1
skin cancer	1/-	-/-	-/-	1/-
ulcers	1/1	1/2	-/-	2/3
heart trouble	-/3	1/2	-/-	1/5
tumors	1/-	2/-	1/-	4/-
dysentery	1/-	-/-	-/-	1/-
hemorrhage (wherein reproductive organs were at risk)	1/-	-/1	-/-	1/1
hypoglycemia	1/-	-/1	-/-	1/1
malaria	1/-	2/1	-/-	3/1
hepatitis	-/-	1/-	-/-	1/-

	M	P	E	TOT YES
polio	-/-	-/1	1/-	1/1
diphtheria	-/-	-/-	1/-	1/-
tuberculosis	-/-	1/1	-/-	1/1
kidney infections	1/-	1/1	-/-	2/1
"terrible sickness"	1/-	1/-	-/-	2/-

	M	P	E	TOT
"pain"	-/1	2/2	-/-	2/3
dangerously high fever	1/1	1/-	1/1	3/2
nicotine addiction	-/1	-/-	-/-	-/1
swollen glands	-/1	-/-	-/-	-/1
burns	-/1	-/-	-/-	-/1
eye problems	-/1	-/-	-/-	-/1
thyroid condition	1/1	1/1	-/-	2/2
mononucleosis	1/-	1/-	1/-	3/-
encephalitis	-/-	1/-	-/-	1/-
infertility	-/-	1/-	-/-	1/-
accidents resulting in permanent loss:	-/-	-/-	-/-	-/-
traumatic head injury	-/-	1/-	-/-	1/-
blindness from head injury	1/-	-/-	-/-	1/-
limbs (arm or leg) badly damaged and irreparable	1/1	-/-	1/2	2/3
near death	2/-	2/1	1/1	5/2

Those healed from basic sicknesses, such as:	M	P	E	TOT
"normal" illness	1/4	3/3	5/9	9/16
"too regular to recollect"	-/1	1/-	2/-	3/1
allergies: elemental and/or food	1/3	-/1	1/-	2/4
back pain	2/2	1/4	2/-	5/6
asthma	1/2	1/1	1/-	3/3
chronic nose bleeds	1/1	-/-	-/-	1/1
migraine headaches	1/1	1/-	-/-	2/1
emotional heartache	2/3	2/-	-/-	4/3
food poisoning	1/-	-/-	-/-	1/-
infections	1/1	1/-	1/2	3/3
gynecological complications	1/1	-/-	-/-	1/1
hernias	-/1	-/-	2/1	2/2
chronic fatigue	-/-	-/-	-/1	-/1

	M	P	E	TOT YES
total of those above who claim to have divine health and strength in addition to having experienced divine healing	2/2	3/1	4/3	9/6
total of those above who claim divine health and strength to the extent that they have never experienced divine healing	2/3	5/1	3/2	10/6

(Note that the sum total of divine healing incident is higher that the sum total of those who were healed. This is because many were healed of more than one disease.)

	M	P	E	TOT NO
Those who have never experienced divine healing	7/8	10/10	19/23	36/41

Question 3. *Have you observed a divine healing?*
n___ y___ If "yes" describe briefly.

_____

_____

(The results of those surveyed, including a comprehensive listing of what they have observed, are as follows)

	M 24/27	P 26/27	E 23/30	TOT YES 73/84
Below are the details of those who responded "yes" "I have seen people divinely healed from . . ."				
tuberculosis and bleeding lungs	1/-	-/2	-/-	1/2
hepatitis	1/-	1/-	-/1	2/1
hemorrhaging	1/-	-/-	-/-	1/-
heart failure/blockage	-/2	-/1	2/-	2/3
terminal cancer	3/4	4/2	3/-	10/6
skin cancer	1/-	1/-	-/-	2/-
cirrhosis-liver problem	-/-	-/-	2/-	2/-
tumors	-/3	-/3	1/2	1/8
lung cancer and smoking	-/-	1/-	-/-	1/-
boils	1/-	-/-	-/-	1/-
collapsed lung	-/-	1/-	-/-	1/-
cysts on ovaries	-/-	1/-	-/-	1/-
cysts in the ear	-/-	1/-	-/1	1/1
critical ear infection	-/-	-/-	1/-	1/-
kidney stones	-/1	1/1	-/-	1/2
appendicitis	-/-	1/-	-/-	1/-
arthritis	-/-	1/1	-/-	1/1
paralysis (1/2 of face)	-/1	1/-	-/-	1/1
cystic fibrosis	-/-	-/-	1/-	1/-

	M	P	E	TOT YES
multiple sclerosis	-/1	-/-	-/-	-/1
spina bifida	-/-	-/-	-/1	-/1
burns	-/-	-/-	-/1	-/1
encephalitis	1/-	-/-	-/-	1/-
cerebral palsy	-/-	-/-	1/-	1/-
stroke; use of limb(s) restored	1/1	-/-	-/-	1/1
epilepsy	1/-	-/-	1/1	2/1
"pain"	1/5	1/-	1/-	3/5
scoliosis	-/-	-/-	1/-	1/-
cholera	-/-	1/-	-/-	1/-
dehydration	-/-	1/-	-/-	1/-
impending miscarriage	1/-	-/-	-/-	1/-
severe burns	1/-	1/-	-/-	2/-
horrid skin problem	3/1	-/-	-/-	3/1
poisonous reptile and insect bites	2/-	-/-	-/-	2/-
leprosy	-/-	-/-	1/1	1/1
polio	1/-	-/-.	-/1	1/1
withered hand and/or foot	1/-	1/-	-/1	2/1
lame	2/-	-/-	-/-	2/-
deaf	-/-	1/-	-/2	1/2
blind (mild cataract to complete blindness)	1/2	2/-	4/1	7/3
deformative gum disease	-/-	1/-	-/-	1/-
diabetes	1/-	-/-	1/1	2/1
uneven leg length	1/-	-/-	1/1	2/1
overt demonic oppression	2/2	-/-	-/1	2/3

	M	P	E	TOT YES
alcoholism and rage in addition to suicidal and homicidal threats	3/-	1/-	-/-	4/-
malaria	-/1	-/-	-/-	-/1
asthma	-/1	-/-	-/-	-/1

chronic fatigue	-/-	-/-	-/1	-/1
ulcers	-/-	-/-	-/1	-/1
infertility	1/2	-/1	-/-	1/3
"innumerable diseases"	5/4	4/-	1/-	10/4
severe illness coinciding with rebellion	1/-	1/-	-/1	2/1
a near death condition	6/3	3/6	3/1	12/10

Basic healings observed are. . .				
"normal" illness	2/3	3/10	7/11	12/24
fever	1/1	1/1	-/-	2/2
strep throat	-/-	1/-	1/-	2/-
pneumonia	1/1	-/-	-/-	1/1
teeth/dental problem	1/-	-/-	-/-	1/-
emotional heartache	-/1	-/3	1/-	1/4
chronic headaches	-/-	2/-	-/-	2/-
infections	1/-	-/1	-/2	1/3

(Note the sum total of divine healing observed is higher than the sum total of those who observed a healing. Many observed more than one divine healing)

	M	P	E	TOT NO
"I have never observed a divine healing"	6/3	4/4	14/12	24/19

Question 4. *Have you been involved in the ministry of divine healing?*

M	P	E	TOT YES
24/21	28/25	28/27	80/73

Below is the breakdown of those who answered "yes." The descriptions listed tell the general overtone of their answers.

"I am regularly involved . . ."	6/9	11/18	1/10	18/37
"I pray for the sick out of obedience"	4/5	6/4	8/8	18/17
"minimally"	12/5	5/3	18/8	35*/16
"yes," but ought to be more involved	2/2	6/-	1/1	9/3

*Over half of the 35 who referred to their involvement in divine healing as minimal talked of a particular event "back when." They had ministered divine healing so irregularly that they could easily list each occasion from their lives by memory. For them it was not a regular and ongoing part of life and ministry.

M	P	E	TOT NO
6/9	2/5	9/15	17/29

Below is the breakdown of those who answered "no." The descriptions listed tell the general overtone of their answers.

	M	P	E	TOT
"no," and I am disturbed about this/wish I were	1/5	-/1	-/2	1/8
"I do not see it as part of my ministry"	5/4	2/4	9/13	16/21

(The following question was given only to educators)

Question 5. *Do you teach divine healing?*

	YES	NO
These educators who aggressively teach divine healing with the goal of imparting this truth to their students.	10/16	
These educators passively teach divine healing, meaning as the topic arose in the biblical text or as students ask questions. For these professors, divine healing is not a subject they avoid but neither do they pursue it.	12/16	
These educators claim that it is not within their subject (not their place) to instruct students in divine healing.		10/3
These educators claim never to have taught about divine healing		5/7*
TOTALS	22/32	15/10

* Of the five professors (seven in 1994) who had never taught divine healing to their students, two (in both surveys) had not instructed for reasons they chose not to disclose. The remaining three (five in 1994) were opposed to divine healing for doctrinal reasons. (These five educators are the ones who answered "negative" to question #1.)

(Question 6 was given only to the educators.)

Question 6. *Is divine healing in the formal curriculum that you see?*

"YES"	15/19
"NO"	22/23

(Question 7 was also only given to the educators.)
Question 7. *What is your stated position on divine healing?*

Of those surveyed, the general breakdown was as follows:

Those with a positive view	21/23
Those with a passive view	11/13
Those with a negative view	5/2

To begin, the 21 with a positive view (23 in 1994) mentioned seven distinct components about divine healing as being for today's church. These are listed below along with the amount they were mentioned. (The greater majority mentioned multiple components.)

It's in the atonement	11/6
God is sovereign and has the prerogative to heal	11/13
Faith is a necessary catalyst	7/3
We are to pray for the sick as commanded in James 5	6/4
I accept and support divine healing	11/7
It is a privilege for the believer	2/3
Sickness is a basis for going to God	2/3

The 11 with a passive view (13 in 1994) offered six differing propositions in support of their position. Almost half of the 11 (13 in 1994) mentioned only one point in summary of their position.

God is sovereign and may withhold healing	7/6
Healing will not be complete until the Second Coming	5/2
Healing is possible	4/5
Healing is available	2/6
Healing cannot be demanded	4/2
Sickness can be chastening and must be accepted	1/4

Below is the breakdown of the five educators (two in 1994) who have a negative view of divine healing:

"Divine healing is not for today and not in the atonement"	4/-
"Divine healing is very rare"	2/1
"I have my doubts about it"	2/2
"Divine healing is not true"	1/-

(The final question about book recommendations was question 5 for missionaries and pastors, question 8 for the educators. Note that the recommendations listed and numbered below are verbatim from the participants response)

TOT = Total, M = Missionary, P = Pastor, E = Educator

Question 8. *What books do you recommend on divine healing?*

BOOK	Breakdown by Vocation				by Ed. level	
	TOT	M	P	E	PhD	NO PhD
K. Bailey, *The Children's Bread*	35/44	9/16	16/20	10/8	10/9	25/35
"No books"	*29/24	10/5	5/4	14/15	13/14	16/10
The Holy Bible	12/14	3/8	6/3	3/3	2/3	10/11
A.B. Simpson, *The Gospel of Healing*	11/12	3/2	5/7	3/3	3/3	8/9
"Simpson's material"	**10/23	4/7	2/8	4/8	3/8	7/15
A.B. Simpson, *The Fourfold Gospel*	8/1	4/-	4/1	-/-	-/-	8/1
Richard M. Sipley, *Understanding Divine Healing*	7/13	1/5	4/4	2/4	2/6	5/7
A.B. Simpson, *The Lord for the Body*	5/4	1/1	2/1	2/2	2/3	3/1

A.J. Gordon, *The Ministry of Healing*	3/4	1/-	1/2	1/2	1/2	2/2
John Wimber, *Power Healing*	3/3	1/1	2/1	-/1	-/1	3/2
Andrew Murray, *Divine Healing*	2/5	-/1	1/2	1/2	1/2	1/3
R.A. Torrey, *Divine Healing*	1/1	-/-	-/1	1/-	1/-	-/1
Becken, *Theology Heilung*	1/-	-/-	-/-	1/-	1/-	-/-
J. Millard Erickson, *Christian Theology*	1/-	-/-	-/-	1/-	1/-	-/-
"Peter Wagner Books"	1/2	-/-	1/-	-/2	-/2	-/-
Ken Blue, *Authority to Heal*	1/1	-/-	-/-	1/1	1/1	
J.R Church, *Divine Healing*	1/-	-/-	-/-	1/-	-/-	1/-
A Loving God and a Suffering World	1/-	-/-	-/-	1/-	-/-	1/-
D. Peters, *James, NIGTC*	1/-	-/-	-/-	1/-	1/-	-/-
Norman Geisler, *Signs and Wonders*	1/-	-/-	-/-	1/-	1/-	-/-
MacMillan, *None of These Diseases*	1/-	-/-	1/-	-/-	-/-	1/-

Kenneth MacKenzie, *Our Physical Heritage in Christ*	1/-	-/-	-/-	1/-	1/-	-/-
C. Shrier, *Divine Health*	1/-	-/-	-/-	1/-	-/-	1/-

* Twenty-nine of 97 is exactly 30 percent of the leaders surveyed (in 1989) who recommend no reading material on the subject of divine healing.

**There was a much greater awareness of Simpson's writings in 1994 than in 1989.

Books That Were Recommended Only in 1994 Survey

	Breakdown by Vocation				by ED Level	
BOOK	TOT	M	P	E	PhD	NO PhD
Frank Stanger, *God's Healing Community*	-/13	-/5	-/4	-/4	-/4	-/9
"The A. W. Tozer Material"	-/5	-/2	-/3	-/-	-/1	-/4
Jack Deere, *Surprised by the Power of the Spirit*	-/3	-/1	-/-	-/2	-/1	-/2
F.F. Bosworth, *Divine Healing*	-/3	-/2	-/-	-/1	-/1	-/2
John Tal Murphree, *A Loving God*	-/2	-/-	-/-	-/2	-/1	-/1
Drake Travis, *Christ Our Healer Today*	-/2	-/-	-/-	-/2	-/1	-/1

"A book by Ron Bliz"	-/1	-/-	-/-	-/1	-/1	-/-
"A book written in Portuguese back in my office in Brazil"	-/1	-/1	-/-	-/-	-/-	-/1
"A book by Roland Brown"	-/1	-/-	-/-	-/1	-/1	-/-
"The C&MA's recommended reading"	-/1	-/-	-/1	-/-	-/-	-/1
Gilquist, *Let's Quit Fighting About the Holy Spirit*	-/1	-/-	-/1	-/-	-/-	-/1
"Books written in Indonesian about divine healing"	-/1	-/1	-/-	-/-	-/-	-/1
Charles Kraft, *Christianity with Power*	-/1	-/-	-/-	-/1	-/-	-/1
Martin Lloyd-Jones, Healing and the Scriptures	-/1	-/-	-/1	-/-	-/-	-/1
"Francis MacNutt's Books"	-/1	-/-	-/-	-/1	-/1	-/-
Leanne Payne, *The Healing Presence*	-/1	-/-	-/-	-/1	-/1	-/-
Ken Sande, *The Peacemaker*	-/1	-/-	-/-	-/1	-/1	-/-
Scanlon, *Inner Healing*	-/1	-/-	-/-	-/1	-/1	-/-
David Seamands, *Healing for Damaged Emotions*	-/1	-/-	-/-	-/1	-/1	-/-
Ruth Stapleton, *Love, Medicine and Miracles*	-/1	-/-	-/-	-/1	-/1	-/-
Phil Yancey, *Disappointment with God*	-/1	-/-	-/-	-/1	-/1	-/-

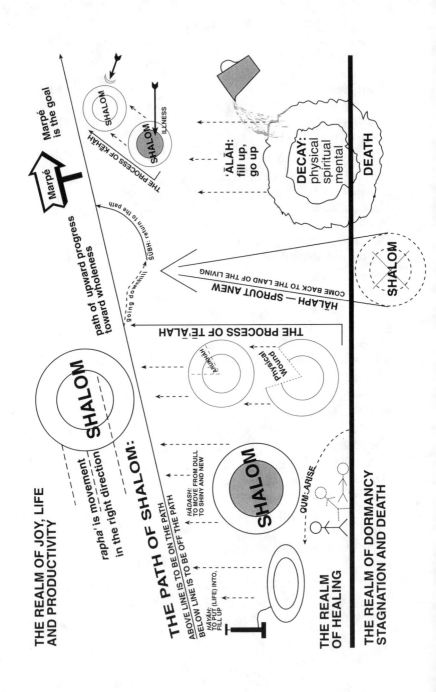

Recommended Reading

Bailey, Keith. *Divine Healing: The Children's Bread.* Harrisburg, PA: Christian Publications, Inc., 1977.

Bartleman, Frank. *Azusa Street.* South Plainfield, NJ: Bridge Publishing, Inc., 1980.

Baxter, J. Sidlow. *Divine Healing of the Body.* Grand Rapids, MI: Zondervan, 1979.

Blue, Ken. *Authority to Heal.* Downers Grove, IL: InterVarsity Press, 1987.

Cho, Paul Yonggi. *The Fourth Dimension.* Plainfield, NJ: Logos International, 1979.

Deere, Jack. *Surprised by the Power of the Spirit.* Grand Rapids, MI: Zondervan, 1993.

Gordon, A.J. *The Ministry of Healing.* 1882 Reprint. Harrisburg, PA: Christian Publications, Inc.. n.d.

Green, Michael. *I Believe in the Holy Spirit.* London: Hodder & Stoughton, 1975.

Harper, Michael. *The Healings of Jesus*. The Jesus Library, ed. Michael Green. Downers Grove, IL: InterVarsity, 1986.

Hartzfeld, David F. and Charles Nienkirchen, eds. *The Birth of a Vision*. Alberta, Canada: Buena Book Services, 1986.

MacNutt, Francis. *Healing*. Notre Dame, IN: Ave Maria Press, 1974.

MacKenzie, Kenneth. *Our Physical Heritage in Christ*. New York: Fleming H. Revell, 1923.

Mayhue, Richard. *Divine Healing Today*. Winona Lake, IN: BMH Books, 1983.

Murray, Andrew. *Divine Healing*. Fort Washington, PA: Christian Literature Crusade, n.d; reprint, Springdale, PA: Whitaker House, 1982.

Murray, Andrew. *The Believer's Full Blessing of Pentecost*. Minneapolis: Bethany House Publishers, 1984.

Niklaus, Robert L., John S. Sawin and Samuel J. Stoesz. *All for Jesus*. Camp Hill, PA: Christian Publications, Inc., 1986.

Oerter, J.H. *Divine Healing in the Light of Scriptures*. Brooklyn, NY: Christian Alliance Publishing Co., 1900.

Seybold, Klaus and Ulrich B. Mueller. *Sickness and Healing*. Translated by Douglas W. Scott. Nashville, TN: Abingdon, 1981.

Simpson, A.B. *The Fourfold Gospel*. Harrisburg, PA: Christian Publications, 1986.

Simpson, A.B. *The Gospel of Healing*. Camp Hill, PA: Christian Publications, Inc.., 1915, reprint 1986.

Sipley, Richard M. *Understanding Divine Healing*. Camp Hill, PA: Christian Publications, Inc, 1990.

Trench, Richard C. *Notes on the Miracles of our Lord*. London: Macmillan & Co., 1978.

Wagner, C. Peter. *Your Spiritual Gifts Can Help Your Church Grow*. Ventura, CA: Regal Books, 1983.

Wilkinson, John. *Health and Healing*. Edinburgh: Handsel, 1980.

Bibliography of Sources

Bailey, Keith. *Divine Healing: The Children's Bread*. Harrisburg, PA: Christian Publications, Inc., 1977.

Blue, Ken. *Authority to Heal*. Downers Grove, IL: InterVarsity Press, 1987.

Brown, Colin, ed. *The New International Dictionary of New Testament Theology*, vol. 2 (G-Pre). Grand Rapids, MI: Zondervan, 1977. s.v. "Heal," by F. Graber and D. Muller.

Buttrick, George Arthur, ed. *The Interpreter's Dictionary of the Bible*, vol. 2 (E-J). Nashville, TN: Abingdon Press, 1962. s.v. "Healing, Health," by R.K. Harrison.

Childs, Brevard S. *The New Testament as Canon: An Introduction*. Philadelphia: Fortress Press, 1984.

Cullman, Oscar. *Christ and Time*. Translated by Floyd F. Filson. Philadelphia: Westminster Press, 1964.

Davids, Peter H. *The Epistle of James*. Grand Rapids, MI: William B. Eerdmans Publishing Company, 1982.

Douglas, Mary, *Purity and Danger*. London: Routledge and Kegan Paul, 1966.

Erickson, Millard J. *Christian Theology*, 3 vols. Grand Rapids, MI: Baker Book House, 1983.

223

Ferguson, Everett, *Backgrounds in Early Christianity*.
Grand Rapids, MI: William B. Eerdmans Publishing
Company, 1987.

Fitzmyer, Joseph A. *The Gospel According to Luke*, 2 vols.
Garden City, NY: Doubleday & Company Inc., 1981.

Furnish, Victor Paul. *II Corinthians*. Garden City, NY:
Doubleday & Company, Inc., 1984.

Gordon, A.J. *The Ministry of Healing*. 1882 Reprint.
Harrisburg, PA: Christian Publications, Inc., n.d.

Gruenler, Royce Gordon. *New Approaches to Jesus and the
Gospels*. Grand Rapids, MI: Baker Book House, 1982.

Harper, Michael. *The Healings of Jesus*, The Jesus Library, ed. Michael Green. Downers Grove, IL: Inter-
Varsity Press, 1986.

Hartzfeld, David F. and Charles Nienkirchen, eds.
The Birth of a Vision. Alberta, Canada: Buena Book
Services, 1986.

Kelsey, Morton T. *Christianity as Psychology: The Healing Power of the Christian Message*. Minneapolis:
Augsburg Publishing House, 1986.

Kraft, Charles. *Christianity with Power: Your Worldview
and Your Experience of the Supernatural*. Ann Arbor, MI:
Vine Books, Servant Publications, 1989.

Ladd, George Eldon. *Jesus and the Kingdom*. New York:
Harper & Row, 1964; reprinted, *The Presence of the Future*. Grand Rapids, MI: William B. Eerdmans Publishing Co., 1981.

Lang, Bernhard, ed. *Anthropological Approaches to the Old Testament,* "The Abominations of Levit-icus," pp. 100-116. Philadelphia: Fortress Press, 1985.

Leupold, H.C. *Exposition of Genesis*, vol. 2. Grand Rapids, MI: Baker Book House, 1942.

Lewis, C.S. *God in the Dock*. Grand Rapids, MI: Eerdmans Publishing Company, 1970.

_____. *Mere Christianity*. New York: Macmillan Publishing Company, 1943; reprint 1952.

_____. *Miracles*. New York: Macmillan Publishing Company, 1947, reprint, 1960.

Lloyd-Jones, Martyn. *Healing and the Scriptures*. Nashville, TN: Oliver Nelson, 1988.

MacKenzie, Kenneth. *Our Physical Heritage In Christ*. New York: Fleming H. Revell, 1923.

MacNutt, Francis. *Healing*. Notre Dame, IN: Ave Maria Press, 1974.

_____. *The Power to Heal*. Notre Dame, IN: Ave Maria Press, 1977.

_____. *The Prayer That Heals*. Notre Dame, IN: Ave Maria Press, 1981.

Marshall, I. Howard. *Luke: Historian and Theologian*. Grand Rapids, MI: Zondervan, 1970.

_____. "The Hope of a New Age: the Kingdom of God in the New Testament." *Themelios*, vol. 11, no. 1 (September 1985), 5-15.

Martin, Ralph P. *James*. Word Biblical Commentary; vol. 48. Waco, TX: Word Books, 1986.

_____ . *2 Corinthians*. Word Biblical Commentary; vol. 40. Waco, TX: Word Books, 1986.

McCant, Jerry. "Paul's Thorn of Rejected Apostleship," *New Testament Studies* 34 (October 1988), 550-572.

McCrossan, T.J. *Bodily Healing and the Atonement*. Seattle: By the author, 1930; reprint, Tulsa, OK: Faith Library Publishers, 1982.

Meyer, Marvin W. *Who Do People Say I Am?* Grand Rapids, MI: William B. Eerdmans Publishing Company, 1983.

Murray, Andrew. *Divine Healing*. Fort Washington, PA: Christian Literature Crusade, n.d.; reprint 1900; reprint, Springdale, PA: Whitaker House, 1982.

Niklaus, Robert L., John S. Sawin and Samuel J. Stoesz. *All for Jesus*. Camp Hill, PA: Christian Publications, Inc., 1986.

Oerter, J.H. *Divine Healing in the Light of Scriptures*. Brooklyn, NY: Christian Alliance Publishing Co., 1900.

Perrin, Norman. *Rediscovering the Teaching of Jesus*. New York: Harper & Row, 1976.

Simpson, A.B. *The Fourfold Gospel*. Harrisburg, PA: Alliance Publishers, 1925, update, edit and reprint, Camp Hill, PA: Christian Publications Inc., 1984.

_____ . *The Gospel of Healing*. Harrisburg, PA: Christian Publications, Inc., 1915; revision, edit and reprint, Camp Hill, PA: Christian Publications Inc., 1986.

_____ . *The Lord for the Body*. New York: Christian Alliance Publishing Company, 1925, reprint, Harrisburg, PA: 1964, 1972, 1973, 1976.

Smith, Oswald J. *The Great Physician*. New York: Christian Alliance Publishing Company, 1927.

Soards, Marion L. *The Apostle Paul: An Introduction to His Writings and Teaching*. New York: Paulist Press, 1987.

Stronstad, Roger. *The Charismatic Theology of St. Luke*. Peabody, MA: Hendrickson Publishers, 1984.

Thompson, A.E. *A.B. Simpson*. Harrisburg, PA: Christian Publications, Inc., 1960.

Trench, Richard C. *Notes on the Miracles of Our Lord*. London: Macmillan & Co., 1978.

Wenham, Gordon. *The Book of Leviticus*. Grand Rapids, MI: William B. Eerdmans Publishing Company, 1979; reprint, 1985.

White, John. *When the Spirit Comes with Power*. Downers Grove, IL: InterVarsity Press, 1988.

Wimber, John. *Power Healing*. San Francisco, CA: Harper & Row, 1987.

About the Author

Drake Travis received his B.A. in biblical literature from Simpson College and his M.A. in literature (New Testament) from Alliance Theological Seminary. He received the President's Cup upon graduation from Simpson College for having the most positive influence on colleagues during his years on campus.

He now serves as the pastor of Salt Company, a college group at Central Washington University that has grown from 25 to over 600 students. He is ordained by The Christian and Missionary Alliance and is an associate pastor for the Alliance church in Ellensburg, Washington. Drake's mission work, travel and studies have taken him to thirty-five of fifty states and to fifteen countries around the world. He and his wife Marlene have three children.